OVERVIEW

Overview

Strategy refers to the direction an organization or business unit takes to achieve its vision, mission, and goals. Organizational strategies include strategies at the corporate, business, and functional levels.

Strategic thinking is essential at all levels, including functional levels. It equips functional managers and departmental leaders to make long-term decisions that align with their organizations' corporate and business strategies, encourages new ways of thinking, and overcomes the constraints associated with having limited information. In effect, it contributes to their success.

Strategic thinking has five main characteristics. It's focused on an organization's strategic vision, involves adopting a systems view, takes a long-term approach, involves being ready to take advantage of opportunities, and considers the past and present.

Traits of strategic thinkers typically include flexibility, openness, a positive outlook, curiosity, future focus, and an ability to identify connections and patterns. Common barriers to thinking strategically include unchallenged assumptions, knowledge that's no longer relevant, reliance on what worked in the past, rigidity, linearity, closed-mindedness, and framing.

Anyone can develop the ability to think strategically and to do this you can carry out certain steps. Develop a clear vision by speaking to senior management and peers, collaborating with individuals, setting priorities, and making trade-offs.

To think strategically, you also have to think creatively. You can learn to do this by regularly challenging assumptions, visualizing possibilities, and participating in creative endeavors.

You also have to be prepared to deal with complexity. You need to adopt a big picture view of your organization, be able to recognize trends and patterns, and align your ideas with strategic objectives. You need to become aware of what's going on across your organization and in its broader environment.

To think strategically and see the bigger picture, it's important to understand both the external and internal contexts of your organization. You can use Porter's model of five forces to help you understand and assess your organization's external environment.

To understand the internal context in which you operate, you need to understand your organization's strategic goals and direction, and how your department can align with these. You should also identify potential stakeholders, gather their input on potential actions, and ensure you consider the impact of your decisions on them.

A big-picture perspective enables you to create a mental model of the complete system of value creation within your organization. You can understand the value chain in terms of Porter's primary and support activities.

The value chain focuses on meeting customer demand, whereas the supply chain focuses on creating a product from supplies. Diagrams of these processes provide an o to create products or services that a customer values.

Another high-level diagram that promotes a big-picture perspective is the SIPOC diagram, which maps out suppliers, inputs, the process, outputs, and customers. Using a SIPOC diagram can help you identify key connections, stakeholders, inputs, and dependencies across an organization.

Having a strategic mind-set involves envisioning what an organization can and should become, and translating organizational objectives into departmental objectives. It also involves taking the future, as well as internal and external environmental factors, into account.

To develop a strategic mind-set, you should clarify objectives, learn to anticipate what may happen in the future, broaden your range of strategic inputs, and widen your perspective on your business and industry.

Analyzing information effectively can help you make better decisions and develop effective solutions to problems. It also supports strategic thinking.

Using information effectively involves determining the kind of information you need to analyze; identifying relationships, patterns, and trends; and balancing intuition with analysis.

SWOT analysis is a useful tool for supporting strategic thinking. It involves assessing an organization's or department's strengths, weaknesses, opportunities, and threats. SWOT analysis can bring focus and discipline to the way you think. It also encourages thinking that's not too structured, and can help you develop a big picture view of your organization and industry.

As a functional manager, you'll often have to make trade-offs. These are situations in which you choose one option over another because it's the best option for your specific situation.

To make effective trade-offs, you should prioritize actions that align with your organization's strategy and objectives. You need to identify and evaluate all alternatives, considering their pros and cons and their likely short- and long-term effects. You also have to balance your department's needs with your organization's needs, ensuring decisions you make won't have a negative impact on other units.

Creative thinking is sometimes perceived as frivolous, but it can be a valuable addition to strategic thinking. It can help you find new and innovative solutions. To think creatively, you need to challenge your assumptions, view things differently, and learn by asking questions.

Challenging your assumptions involves challenging your current approaches to work, recognizing and examining your assumptions, welcoming new ideas, and changing your routines. To view things differently, you can ask probing questions, work counterculturally, reframe problems as opportunities, and use lateral thinking tools. Learning by asking questions involves obtaining views from others in your organization and asking open-ended questions.

DEVELOPING THE CAPACITY TO THINK STRATEGICALLY

Developing the Capacity to Think Strategically

Strategy combines thoughts, ideas, insights, experiences, goals, expertise, perceptions, and expectations to provide a framework and guidance for specific actions. In the context of this course, strategy is the direction of an organization or business unit. It's how the organization achieves its vision, mission, and goals.

In an organization, different strategies are used at different levels. Collectively these strategies are referred to as organizational strategies. They include corporate-level strategies, business-level strategies, and functional-level strategies.

Thinking strategically means you look outward, address environmental factors, take a long-term view, and consider a range of stakeholders. So it's a broader way of thinking that doesn't just consider day-to- day level processes, plans, and procedures. Instead, it focuses on the big picture, identifying how each decision and activity can help support organizational goals.

Strategic thinking has specific characteristics that set it apart from other, more linear ways of thinking and operating in business.

Strategic thinkers add value to their organizations by virtue of their ability to analyze opportunities and problems objectively. They can anticipate the impact of their actions because they know how to weigh up the positives and negatives in a situation, and assess the implications of different actions. Strategic thinkers visualize future possibilities. This enables them to make decisions, take action, and develop fresh approaches to their work.

Strategic thinkers are also able to understand abstract ideas and turn them into more concrete ideas. They formulate a direction for action through thinking. So when dealing with different abstract ideas, strategic thinkers reframe them in terms of concrete actions or decisions.

Even if you have the traits that make for good strategic thinking, you may need to overcome various common barriers. Unchallenged assumptions, knowledge that's no longer relevant, reliance on what worked in the past, rigidity, linearity, closed-mindedness, and framing can all prevent strategic thinking efforts.

Thinking strategically can have several benefits. It can result in better long-term decisions and enhance both your success and the overall success of your organization. But how can you become a strategic thinker?

Before you can think strategically you need to have a clear vision of what the future could or should be. It's this vision that determines your focus and aims, and guides your actions and thinking.

The vision you develop should directly support and align with your organization's overall strategic vision. So an important step is gaining a good understanding of what your organization's vision is.

Creative thinking helps you avoid conformity, or reliance on what's simply accepted. You learn to develop and explore new ideas, and different ways of responding to and completing tasks. It also involves being open and ready to change your views about how things should work. This makes it easier to develop new processes or products, or better methods to serve customers.

A final way to develop your strategic thinking ability is to make sure you know what's going on across your organization and its environment. This requires you look outside your department and assess both the organization's internal and external environments. Useful information you gather could relate to new ideas and trends, changes in customer needs, changes in competitive strategies, and internal challenges and changes.

UNDERSTANDING STRATEGY

Understanding strategy

Before a house can be built, a vision is required for how it will look, how it will be developed, and what resources have to be identified, acquired, and used. This vision, plans, and end result are borne out of and driven forward by a broader strategy. The same is true in business, where strategy is required to move a vision and its related plans forward.

As you may have noted, there's no set definition for the term strategy. It can mean different things in different industries and organizations, or even between different departments of the same organization.

Strategy combines thoughts, ideas, insights, experiences, goals, expertise, perceptions, and expectations to provide a framework and guidance for specific actions.

In the context of this course, strategy is the direction of an organization or business unit. It's how the organization achieves its vision, mission, and goals.

In an organization, different strategies are used at different levels. Collectively these strategies are referred to as organizational strategies. They include corporate-level strategies, business-level strategies, and functional-level strategies.

See each level of strategy to find out more about it.

Corporate-level strategies

Corporate-level strategies involve top management and affect an organization as a whole. They're concerned with the course an organization takes over a long term, generally of three or more years. They may deal with social, economic, legal, political, or technological factors that form part of the external business environment.

For example, corporate-level strategies determine what businesses an organization should compete in and how these should be coordinated or developed. They also determine how organizational structure should be established to support the organization's direction.

Business-level strategies

Business-level strategies take a narrower view than those at the corporate level. They focus on the individual strategic business units, or SBUs, that make up an organization. Examples of SBUs are divisions, product lines, or units that can be managed independently from other business units.

Business-level strategies are usually developed by middle-level managers and extend over a period of one to three years. Examples of business-level strategies include SBU diversification, integration, and divestment, as well as monitoring products and markets, determining what products to introduce in a new market, and determining how each SBU can secure and sustain a competitive advantage.

Functional-level strategies

Functional strategies, also called departmental or tactical strategies, are aligned with corporate and business strategic goals. They deal with the main functions of the organization or the SBUs such as marketing and sales, finance and accounting, productions, operations, human resources, administration, and IT.

Functional managers at mid to low levels, and departmental leaders and professionals typically develop these strategies. Functional-level strategies relate to business processes and the value chain, and operations necessary to design, produce, sell, supply, and service products or services. They also include quality control of products and services, and strategies for customer relationship and marketing management.

Understanding different levels of strategies helps you recognize the synergistic relationships among different parts of an organization.

This is an important element in strategic thinking – understanding how the parts contribute to the whole.

Question

Match each strategy level to a corresponding example.

Options:

A. Functional-level strategy

B. Corporate-level strategy

C. Business-level strategy

Targets:

1. Developing a strategy for dealing with customer complaints for incorrect invoices

2. Deciding what portfolio of businesses a company should be involved in

3. Determining what products the small business division in a retail bank should develop and introduce over the next year

Answer:

Functional-level, or departmental, strategies relate to individual departments or SBUs. An example is a strategy for managing customer relationships.

Corporate-level strategies affect an organization as a whole and relate to decisions like which type of businesses the organization should pursue.

Business-level strategies deal with individual SBUs and how they can support corporate-level goals. For example, they focus on decisions such as which products to introduce into specific segments.

UNDERSTANDING STRATEGIC THINKING

Understanding strategic thinking

It's common to associate the term strategic thinking with the higher levels of organizational strategy and with top-level executives. However, it's also important for operational, or functional, managers to engage in strategic thinking.

Thinking strategically means you look outward, address environmental factors, take a long-term view, and consider a range of stakeholders. So it's a broader way of thinking that doesn't just consider day-to- day level processes, plans, and procedures. Instead, it focuses on the big picture, identifying how each decision and activity can help support organizational goals.

For functional managers, strategic thinking is a skill and toolset used to analyze opportunities and problems from a broader perspective. It can also help functional managers understand the connections between their day-to-day work and their organization, its strategic goals, and business environment.

Ultimately, strategic thinking results in better decision making and management of specific departments or business units.

Question

Strategic thinking is the same as operational thinking – both focus on putting best practices in place to contribute to short-term competitive advantage.

Do you think this statement is true or false?

Options:

1. True
2. False

Answer:

Actually, strategic thinking and operational thinking are different. Strategic thinking takes a broader, more long-term perspective than operational thinking.

Strategic thinking is sometimes confused with operational thinking or with strategic planning. It's important to understand how strategic thinking differs from these concepts.

See each concept to learn how it differs from strategic thinking.

Operational thinking

Operational thinking is about putting best practices in place to create value by reducing costs, performing activities more efficiently than competitors, working quickly, and making incremental improvements to procedures. This may be good for the short-term competitive advantage but doesn't do much for long-term growth as competing companies start to imitate one another.

Strategic thinking, however, considers how to do things differently from competitors so that what's offered is unique. This results in innovation and creates long-term, sustainable competitive advantage.

Strategic planning

Once strategies have been identified, they need to be implemented. This is when strategic planning is used. It's an analytical, linear process for determining what steps to follow, and in what order, to implement a strategy.

Strategic thinking, however, requires intuition and creativity, and isn't strictly linear. It involves assessing decisions in relation to a whole organization and its environment, and identifying opportunities as they arise. So instead of determining how to implement a strategy, it involves identifying what strategy is suitable and what its likely effects will be.

Consider an example of how strategic thinking is used.

A government's agency provides over 100 services to the public through a network of office locations. These services include depositing local taxes, as well as handling land registry, vehicle registration, and driving licenses, personal property registry, and corporate registrations.

However, there's pressure on the agency's infrastructure, resulting in long waiting times and customer dissatisfaction. With recent changes in the political and economic landscape, the current government is attempting to improve efficiency, service, and customer satisfaction in all its operations.

Two managers, Andrea and Curtis, head two key departments in the organization. They have different ways of thinking about the organization and about their individual departments.

See each manager to find out more about the management approaches of Andrea and Curtis.

Andrea

Andrea regularly assesses the changing economic and political environment in the region and how they impact her organization and department. She reads the corporate newsletter, analyses in the media, strategic communications such as quarterly reports, and top management's analyses of her organization's performance. She also takes note of key executive decisions and speaks to her bosses to gain more clarity on their priorities.

Based on what Andrea thinks the future holds for her organization, she determines her department needs to invest more in technology and training so it can improve its customer service. She prepares her team, takes all possible steps to improve customer service with existing resources, and submits a request for required resources to top managers. She also identifies an opportunity for her employees in the form of a third-party company that specializes in customer service training.

Curtis

Curtis puts a lot of effort into motivating his team to achieve his department's day-to-day goals. His focus is on maintaining a high level of quality and efficiency. He investigates opportunities for improving internal processes and takes steps to ensure each employee in his department is happy and dedicated.

Curtis focuses on resolving operational issues and has little time for analyzing what's happening outside his area of work.

In the example, Andrea is the strategic thinker. She assesses circumstances that arise outside her immediate area of work and takes steps to align her department's activities to the organization's overall goals. In your role, you may face difficult decisions that require you to examine a situation from a broad perspective and develop solutions that benefit your organization.

Thinking strategically can have several benefits:

*   it equips you to make smart long-term decisions that are aligned with the decisions of others,
*   it can contribute to your own success by ensuring you align your goals with business and corporate-level strategies,
*   it helps you foster new ways of thinking, and
*   it can help you overcome limitations associated with having only a limited amount of information.

See each benefit of thinking strategically to learn more about it.

Make smart long-term decisions

Thinking strategically ensures you make decisions in context, assessing how they'll affect your entire organization – as well as individual functional areas – over the long term. The result is better decisions that contribute to overall organizational success.

Contribute to your success

Thinking strategically means you're aware of the business and corporate-level strategies that exist in your organization. This awareness means you're better able to lead your department or team in a direction that aligns with the overall direction of your organization. In turn, this will make you more successful in your role.

Foster new ways of thinking

By thinking strategically, you'll be able to encourage a culture that supports creativity and new ways of thinking. You'll help prompt others in your department to draw ideas and inspiration from a broad view of the organization and its environment.

Overcome limitations

Thinking strategically means looking at your organization and the business environment in which it operates from a broad perspective. This enables you to think of and anticipate issues that exist outside your area of influence. This lets you overcome constraints associated with having only a limited amount of information and a limited view of the forces that lie outside your influence.

Question

What are some of the benefits of strategic thinking?

Options:

1. It enables you to make better short-term decisions that affect your department

2. It promotes a culture that supports innovation

3. It enables you to anticipate circumstances that exist outside your area of influence

4. It enables you to run your department successfully without the need to align the department's direction with corporate-level strategies

Answer:

Option 1: This option is incorrect. A benefit of strategic thinking is that it equips you to make better long-term decisions that align with the decisions of other departments, and with your organization's overall vision and goals.

Option 2: This is a correct option. Strategic thinking encourages creativity and new ways of thinking, with ideas and inspiration drawn from a larger view of an organization and its environment.

Sorin Dumitrascu

Option 3: This option is correct. Thinking strategically means having a broad perspective of your organization and the environment in which it operates. This makes it easier to consider and anticipate issues that exist outside your area of influence.

Option 4: This is an incorrect option. Thinking strategically involves an awareness of business- and corporate-level strategies. This ensures you're better able to lead your department in a direction that's aligned with the overall company direction.

CHARACTERISTICS OF STRATEGIC THINKING

Characteristics of strategic thinking

Strategic thinking has specific characteristics that set it apart from other, more linear ways of thinking and operating in business.

Strategic thinking has five main characteristics.

A focus on strategic vision

An important characteristic of strategic thinking is that it's focused on a vision. In the context of this course, this is the vision of an organization's leadership, which defines the organization's direction and what it aims to achieve and become.

It's this vision that determines what the organization's goals and objectives are. It can also give all employees a sense that they're working toward something and are part of a bigger plan.

To develop the ability to think strategically, you need to put the organizational vision and goals at the heart of each decision you make.

This is so that the decisions and activities of functional units, or departments, align with and support the organization's strategic vision and goals.

In the example involving Andrea and Curtis and the government agency, the agency's strategic vision is to become a truly customer-focused organization that delivers exemplary service.

Andrea decides to explore several innovative ways to align herself and her department with the organization's vision:

- she seeks direct customer feedback and encourages team members to identify customers' expectations of her department, as well as how far the department's services meet those expectations,
- she engages a professional market research agency to design and administer a survey and focus group to clearly identify the needs of customers,
- she personally reviews customer complaints and service escalations, and
- she motivates, encourages, and rewards exemplary service by her team members.

A systems view

Strategic thinking involves adopting a systems view of an organization. This means considering all decisions and activities in relation to a bigger picture, considering how the various parts of an organization link and work together within the organization's broader business environment.

It also helps you determine your role in the organization's supply chain.

This systems view of an organization enables you to understand how your decisions and day-to-day actions affect, and are affected by, internal and external stakeholders in other parts of the organization and environment.

For instance, while conducting a supply chain analysis of the organization, Andrea realizes the importance of her department to other departments and the organization as a whole in delivering services to customers.

Andrea's big picture view makes her aware of how the organization's priorities change with changing government priorities.

For instance, she can sense the changing socio-political and economic environment in which her organization operates, giving her time to refocus her priorities and take proactive steps for making her department more customer focused and efficient.

A long-term approach

To think strategically, you need to take a long-term approach. You need to consider how each decision and action you take may add value to your organization over the long term – rather than focusing on short-term gains or quick fixes.

A long-term approach helps you develop long-term competitive advantages for your organization.

In the example involving Curtis and Andrea, Curtis is a conscientious manager – but he's perhaps focused too much on achieving the short-term, day-to-day goals for his department.

Andrea, however, is aware of the long-term direction of her organization. She doesn't think just about the organization's current goals, but is interested in the direction it will take over a number of years.

She recognizes her department's long-term direction and how it's affected because she follows the strategic vision, directions, and goals of her organization's leadership. She also stays informed by reading various management or media analyses and following news.

As a result of Andrea's long-term view, she's able to start preparing herself and her department appropriately.

She communicates her long-term view with her key team members to keep them informed and have their support. They then start focusing on what customers want and what will improve customer satisfaction with her department's services.

She also identifies gaps in people, process, and technology areas that are challenging her department's ability to deliver superior customer service. She works on these gaps, and communicates challenges and progress made to her bosses, making requests from them for resources where needed.

Readiness to take advantage of opportunities

Strategic thinking involves being ready to identify and take advantage of any opportunities to further your organization's strategic vision and goals.

As you begin to develop the capacity to think strategically, you'll be more aware of what's going on inside and outside the organization and be quicker to recognize unanticipated opportunities to further, or even redirect, a strategy.

Andrea, for instance, recognizes an opportunity to improve her department's ability to provide better customer service by using an outside trainer.

Often it's taking advantage of opportunities that arise in the external environment that sets organizations apart from their competitors.

Being aware of your organization's culture and how it functions, and of the relationships between different departments or areas, can also help you recognize opportunities.

Consideration of past and present

Strategic thinking looks to the past. The past gives context, and considering it and learning from the past can help you make better decisions in the future.

For example, examining the past behaviors of important stakeholders, such as other departments in your organization, customers, or suppliers, can help you anticipate how they will respond to new ideas and strategies.

Strategic thinking also requires consideration of the present because it places constraints on what you can achieve.

Thinking strategically can lead to unconventional and creative ideas. Yet it still draws on reason to select the ideas that make sense, given the context – which the past and present offer clues to.

Strategic thinking, then, is "thinking in time."

Andrea, for instance, does a realistic assessment of her current and future requirements to meet customer service levels she sets for her department. She's confident of support from other departments on shared services based on past experience.

Andrea also adjusts her business case for more technical resources based on her experience of senior management's priorities while taking advantage of the organization's long-term drive for better customer satisfaction.

If you bring together the five characteristics of strategic thinking, what you may come up with is a long- term thinker who visualizes what might or could be, drawing on the past and present contexts.

It's someone who understands how the organization fits within its external environment and how relationships with stakeholders work. And it's someone who is not afraid to take advantage of opportunities.

It takes time to develop the skill of thinking strategically. However, it's an essential skill to have if you want to contribute to achieving your organization's overall goals.

Question

What are some examples of strategic thinking?

Options:

1. A functional manager makes it a priority to set long-term goals for her department, regardless of the effects these have on other departments

2. An operations manager develops departmental goals to boost employee productivity, in line with the organization's vision of doubling its output in the next three years

3. A manager focuses on setting and achieving weekly departmental productivity goals

4. A marketing manager assesses changing trends in his company's client base to better understand how to market new products

Answer:

Option 1: This option is incorrect. Although this manager is considering what the long-term goals of her department should be, she needs to have a systems view of her organization. This requires assessing how her department goals and actions affect, and are affected by, other departments within the organization.

Option 2: This option is correct. A characteristic of strategic thinking is that it's focused on an organization's overall strategic vision. Functional managers who think strategically align their departments' goals with the vision and goals of the organization as a whole.

Option 3: This is an incorrect option. Strategic thinking involves aligning departmental goals and efforts with the long-term strategic vision and goals of an organization – rather than setting and focusing on departmental goals in isolation.

Option 4: This is a correct option. When functional managers think strategically, they're aware of and consider the external business environment and any opportunities it provides for supporting an organization's vision and goals.

STRATEGIC THINKER TRAITS

Strategic thinker traits

Are you a strategic thinker? Before you can answer this question, you should be able to answer "yes" to a set of specific questions. For example, do you consider what's going on around you - in your unit, company, industry, and wider business environment? Do you look for opportunities that might give good results in the future? Are you good at visualizing new possibilities? Your answers may help you to determine whether you have the skills and traits of a strategic thinker.

Strategic thinkers add value to their organizations by virtue of their ability to analyze opportunities and problems objectively. They can anticipate the impact of their actions because they know how to weigh up the positives and negatives in a situation, and assess the implications of different actions. Strategic thinkers visualize future possibilities. This enables them to make decisions, take action, and develop fresh approaches to their work.

Strategic thinkers are also able to understand abstract ideas and turn them into more concrete ideas. They formulate a direction for action through thinking. So when dealing with different abstract ideas, strategic thinkers reframe them in terms of concrete actions or decisions.

They also trust their intuition and know how to use it constructively. Distrusting your intuition really means you distrust the knowledge you have developed through experience. But intuition is an important element in strategic thinking - one that can lead to creative leaps in thought.

And strategic thinkers understand the cause-and-effect linkages that occur in the different situations, processes, and projects they have to deal with.

These are skills that can be learned and honed, and they're related to certain personal traits and behaviors that successful strategic thinkers have. These traits include flexibility, openness, a positive outlook, curiosity, future focus, and an ability to identify connections and patterns.

See each trait to learn more about it.

Flexibility

Flexibility is the ability to change your approach and ideas when new situations or information demand this. Strategic thinking is a dynamic process of synthesizing stimuli from the internal and external environments to create a holistic perspective of the organization. External situations change, and strategic thinkers are able to adapt their thinking accordingly.

Openness

Openness refers to your readiness to accept new ideas, as well as criticism, from your supervisors, coworkers, and external customers, suppliers, and other partners. Strategic thinkers realize that different perspectives and opinions are valuable for viewing situations from different angles, and making prudent and objective decisions.

Positive outlook

Having a positive outlook means being able to recognize difficulties and challenges as potential opportunities, and believing in a positive outcome. Strategic thinkers know they're not always in control of the circumstances they need to navigate. A good attitude that enables them to keep their eyes on the goal is what's needed to maintain forward thinking in difficult situations.

Curiosity

Curiosity in this context refers to your level of interest in the affairs of your department, organization, and industry. Strategic thinking places a priority on being as informed and knowledgeable as possible, so you have a better framework within which to analyze and assess the situations you face.

Future focus

Future focus refers to the foresight you're able to show regarding changing situations your organization may have to deal with, as well as valuable opportunities and potential threats. Strategic thinking is concerned with the organization's long-term goals and objectives. Strategic thinkers process the decisions they make, and the actions they take, in the light of the direction the organization is heading and what it's trying to become.

Ability to identify connections

A key trait for strategic thinking is the ability to identify patterns and relationships between different fields of knowledge and expertise, between functional units, and between an organization and its various external factors. This ability will depend on your knowledge and experience. Strategic thinkers take a big picture view of the organization and the parts in its system.

AN EXAMPLE OF A STRATEGIC THINKER

An example of a strategic thinker

Consider Adam who is a branch manager at Central-West Bank. His job is to ensure customers are satisfied, the bank's customer base is growing, operations are profitable, and employees are competent and customer-oriented.

Regional management has challenged all branch managers to find ways to cut operating costs in their respective branches by 10% to meet the organization's goal of increased margins to pursue its expansion plans.

Adam needs to think strategically about the best ways to align his branch's practices and systems with the organization's goals.

Adam's initial response could be to examine the budget and look for ways to cut costs. Instead, he tries to focus on the future and think in terms of the long-term and big picture view. He realizes the goal isn't really cost reduction, but rather improving the margins or the bottom line. Cost reduction is definitely a way to achieve this goal, but it may not be possible to cut 10% without a drop in the service and product quality.

Adam considers the possibility of increasing revenue to achieve the organizational goal of a larger bottom line for his branch. He sets a target of 5% cost reduction and 10% revenue growth – which has the same desired effect on the margins as a straight 10% cost reduction would have. He discusses these goals with his team and his bosses, who seem to approve of the idea.

Adam also decides to talk with peer managers of other branches in his region to find out how they're addressing the situation. He knows that by being willing to collaborate and showing openness, he stands to benefit from the insights and best practices of his peers.

The response of one manager in particular takes Adam by surprise – but makes him think. The manager suggests Adam should be more careful about sharing his ideas too freely because of the competitive rivalry that exists between branch managers vying for promotion.

Unsure how to respond, Adam contacts another branch manager he respects to ask for his opinion. Although the manager agrees that an unhealthy competitive spirit does exist among managers, he feels that an openness to discuss ideas and find ways to work together will be beneficial for all the branches.

Adam agrees that even though it might initially be perceived negatively, creating an open forum to engage the issues together needs to happen. He's positive it won't be long before his colleagues see the benefits for their branches and for themselves.

Question

Match the three strategic thinking traits Adam displayed to the appropriate descriptions from the scenario.

Options:

A. Future focus

B. Openness

C. Positive outlook

Targets:

1. Adam knows that cutting costs for the sake of the budget now might steer the bank further away from its long-term goals if it weakens product or service quality

2. Adam is willing to consult his fellow branch managers to find out how they're dealing with the situation, and takes the opinions offered seriously

3. Adam's realistic about possible negative perceptions, but remains confident that it can be overcome with the right approach

Answer:

Because Adam is future focused, he has the foresight to see how decisions made in the present situation might play out with positive or negative results in the future.

Because Adam is open, he's ready to receive new ideas from his colleagues. When one manager suggests something he wasn't expecting, he considers it and asks for a second opinion.

Even though Adam anticipates a negative response, he doesn't allow it to deter him from pursuing the solution he feels is appropriate.

As he tries to analyze the situation and identify possible connections and options, he realizes the value of his idea isn't just about mutual support and the exchange of ideas.

More-efficiently-run branches throughout the region will result in greater customer satisfaction in general – which will translate into more customers for his branch too.

Adam's curious to think more about how the branches can attract more customers, make them buy more products, and increase the revenue to the desired level. He knows it's necessary to re-ask basic questions like "Why do people come to our bank?" and "What products and services do they need?" Adam knows changes will have to be made, but he's willing to put in the effort to make them happen.

Question

Match the remaining three strategic thinking traits Adam displayed to the appropriate descriptions from the scenario.

Options:

A. Flexibility

B. Curiosity

C. Ability to identify connections

Targets:

1. Adam knows the solution he's suggesting will require changes to be made, but he's willing to do what's necessary

2. Adam's keen to re-explore the answers to basic questions related to the bank's services and clients' motivations for banking with it

3. Adam recognizes the best way to boost business in his own branch is to build a better customer experience in all branches in his region

Answer:

Adam isn't limited by a commitment to processes and structures that might not be helpful anymore. He's willing to be flexible to make changes where appropriate.

Adam's curiosity doesn't allow him to assume he already knows the answers to his questions. He's motivated to re-examine them.

Because Adam is able to identify connections, he can recognize how the performance and success of the other branches have a direct bearing on that of his own.

STRATEGIC THINKING BARRIERS

Strategic thinking barriers

Even if you have the traits that make for good strategic thinking, you may need to overcome various common barriers. Unchallenged assumptions, knowledge that's no longer relevant, reliance on what worked in the past, rigidity, linearity, closed-mindedness, and framing can all prevent strategic thinking efforts.

See each barrier to strategic thinking to learn more about it.

Unchallenged assumptions

Be aware that some of the assumptions you bring to a problem or situation may inhibit strategic thinking. Unchallenged assumptions that prove to be incorrect can waste a lot of time and effort. They may lead your thinking in the wrong direction.

Knowledge that may not be relevant

Times and situations change. Knowledge that may have been relevant and particularly significant in the past may no longer be, given present circumstances and where the organization needs to go in the future.

Reliance on what worked in the past

Past successes can result in an unhealthy reliance on what worked in the past, and limit your ability to adapt and think beyond what's already known.

Experience and insight you've gained from the past are immensely valuable for future planning. However, effective strategic thinking thrives when you use the past and present as context and make imaginative leaps to find new possibilities.

Rigidity

Rigidity is the opposite of flexibility. If your thoughts are too rigid, it means you can't or aren't willing to move beyond what you currently think because you think you're right. However, rigidity in thought is often based in fear of uncertainty and the unknown. Strategic thinking requires flexibility and openness.

Linearity

Linearity is assuming things always happen in a linear sequence. Linear logic is helpful for planning but can be too limited when it comes to solving problems, especially problems that involve connections among multiple variables.

For example, with a linear perspective you might assume that the means determine the end. A more strategic approach might be to consider that the opposite is true – that the required outcome has to determine the means.

Closed-mindedness

Being closed-minded is the opposite to being open to new ideas. It involves assuming you know the answer, no other answer could be correct, and you don't need any other input.

When you think you have the right answer, the tendency is to stop thinking because, in your mind, the job's done. However, forcing yourself to continue thinking can often yield better answers.

Framing

Framing is the belief that specific rules and limitations can restrict the possibilities and solutions you may want to explore. In reality, many of these limitations may be avoidable – or may not actually exist.

For example, a project manager is hesitant to institute necessary process changes because these could add further time pressure to a project. Instead, it may be possible to determine how to implement the changes with minimal impact on the project schedule.

After hearing the concerns of many of his peer managers, Adam decides it's best to get everyone together for a meeting. He hopes that by creating a network for support and collaboration, he might be able to raise enthusiasm levels among his fellow branch managers.

When Adam tries to schedule the meeting, however, he's surprised by the degree of negativity he encounters from many of the other branch managers.

Some of the branch managers immediately shoot down the idea of a meeting, claiming that the solution is simple. Statistics from previous years show that more publicity and advertising means more feet through the door. They just need to rely on what worked in the past.

Others express the opinion that these kinds of meetings are usually a waste of time – time that would be better spent reviewing budgets and past advertising campaigns.

Adam is disappointed by the closed-mindedness and rigidity that seems to characterize many of his peer managers. They seem to want to fall back on tried-and-tested past solutions.

You need to be aware of possible barriers to strategic thinking as you develop the capacity to carry out this type of thinking.

And knowing the traits that support and promote strategic thinking is also important. Strategic thinking requires you to be flexible, open, have a positive outlook, be curious, have a sense of the future, and be able to make connections and see patterns in situations you face.

Case Study: Question 1 of 2

John is a team leader who needs to find ways to improve efficiencies in processes and cut costs.

Answer the questions in order.

Question

What are some of the traits of strategic thinking that John demonstrates?

Options:

1. Flexibility
2. Positive outlook
3. Openness
4. Relying on what worked in the past

Answer:

Option 1: This option is correct. John is flexible to the change indicated by top management and tries to find out as much as he can in order to contribute. He remains flexible.

Option 2: This is a correct option. John is energized by top management's challenge. He recognizes this as an opportunity.

Option 3: This option is incorrect. Openness is a trait of a strategic thinker. By dismissing the idea of a colleague, John shows a lack of openness.

Option 4: This is an incorrect option. Top management has challenged the organization to think differently in order to improve efficiency and cut costs. Relying on what worked in the past may not help and could be a barrier to strategic thinking.

Case Study: Question 2 of 2

What other traits of a strategic thinker does John exemplify?

Options:

1. Ability to identify connections
2. Curiosity
3. Trusting assumptions
4. Sticking to reasonable short-term solutions

Answer:

Option 1: This option is correct. John uses the information he gathers from his friend and from people within the organization to suggest a new system for his project.

Option 2: This is a correct option. John keeps up to date with the industry he's in and in project management. This gives him a better frame in which to assess problems and make decisions for his team.

Option 3: This option is incorrect. This is actually a barrier to strategic thinking. Strategic thinkers challenge their assumptions because these may lead them in the wrong direction.

Option 4: This is an incorrect option. Strategic thinking is future focused. If John had been more future focused, he might have seen the integrated system's potential for laying the foundation for future improvements in efficiencies and costs across the entire organization.

THINKING STRATEGICALLY

Thinking strategically

Thinking strategically can have several benefits. It can result in better long-term decisions and enhance both your success and the overall success of your organization. But how can you become a strategic thinker?

Certain traits, like being open-minded and able to identify patterns and connections, can help you think strategically. You can help to develop these traits and your ability to think strategically by taking specific steps:

- develop a clear vision,
- be creative, which is an essential skill of strategic thinking,
- be prepared to deal with complexity, and
- know what's going on in your organization and its environment.

DEVELOPING A CLEAR VISION

Developing a clear vision

Before you can think strategically you need to have a clear vision of what the future could or should be. It's this vision that determines your focus and aims, and guides your actions and thinking.

The vision you develop should directly support and align with your organization's overall strategic vision. So an important step is gaining a good understanding of what your organization's vision is.

Your organization may have a written document or another resource, like a web site, outlining its vision and mission. So finding this document is a good starting point. In addition, you should speak to managers and colleagues in other departments or functional areas. For instance, if your organization's vision is to be the industry leader in delivering customer value, ask questions to clarify this vision and determine what it means for your department.

To clarify your organization's vision, you can also review various publications – such as statements from the CEO and quarterly reports – and determine how your organization allocates its resources to various value creating activities. In this way, you can gain further insight into what your organization's strategic vision actually means.

Understanding your organization's strategic vision might help you develop and refine your own vision about your department or work. This helps you align your personal vision to your organization's vision so you can succeed in your role.

To determine a clear vision for the future, you must also collaborate with individuals from other groups and functional areas.

Leaders in other departments are likely to have different views of how your organization operates. By seeking to understand their viewpoints and priorities, and how their departments operate, you'll gain a better idea of how your decisions may affect them. You'll also be more likely to gain their support for initiatives you implement.

For example, the manager of a Human Resources, or HR, Department wants to introduce efficiencies into the process of managing HR data. He meets with departmental leaders to get their opinions about a particular software that could help achieve this. By taking a collaborative approach, the manager can gather information and discover which capabilities the software should have and possible implications of the change. He may discover that the departmental leaders support his idea more readily because he's asked for their input.

It's also important to develop a shared understanding of situations with senior management and your team. You want everyone to know what they're working toward and how their efforts are interconnected. This is particularly important when challenges arise. Sharing a common understanding will avoid unnecessary confusion. And given the dynamic challenges facing organizations and the possible sense of disorganization and confusion, this can be an important step in guiding others with focused thinking.

Part of determining a clear vision is determining what your priorities are and being willing to make trade- offs if necessary.

Some priorities may conflict. So you'll need to understand and evaluate the advantages and disadvantages of each possible trade-off.

For example, a product development manager works for an organization that strives to provide high- quality products to its customers. This manager's vision for her department is to continue producing and delivering high-quality products. However, the manager's been asked to prepare for the launch of a new product and to introduce it six weeks ahead of schedule to meet the demands of an important customer.

The product development manager knows that introducing the product earlier may result in poorer quality. She thinks about her priorities and vision, as well as possible trade-offs, and decides to forfeit being ahead of schedule for maintaining quality. She speaks to the customer and assures him that, although she's sticking to the original release date, this will ensure quality isn't compromised.

Question

What is guiding the departmental manager's strategic thinking in this case?

Options:

1. The organization's strategic vision
2. The important customer's expectations

Answer:

Actually, the organization's strategic vision of delivering quality to customers is what's guiding the departmental manager's strategic thinking. For this reason, she's willing to forfeit being ahead of schedule for maintaining product quality.

To determine priorities and acceptable trade-offs, you also need to understand the impact of your decisions on others.

For example, the development manager realizes that if she chooses to introduce the new product ahead of schedule, other departments – such as those involved in purchase and manufacturing – will also be affected.

Question

What can you do to develop a clear vision?

Options:

1. Talk to others about your organization's strategic vision
2. Determine what your priorities are
3. Focus on your department's requirements
4. Verify that you, your team, and your managers have the same understanding of situations
5. Prevent others from influencing your own views
6. Work with other departmental leaders

Answer:

Option 1: This is a correct option. To gain clarity on your organization's strategic vision, it's a good idea to ask senior managers and peers how they perceive and respond to it. Once you're clear about your organization's vision, you can develop your own in line with it.

Option 2: This option is correct. To develop a clear strategic vision, you need to determine what your priorities are and identify any necessary trade-offs.

Option 3: This is an incorrect option. You need to collaborate with individuals or groups outside your department to develop a clear vision that aligns with the overall vision of your organization.

Option 4: This is a correct option. It's important to develop a shared understanding of situations with your team and managers so everyone is clear about what's required and what the goals are.

Option 5: This option is incorrect. To establish a clear vision, you should ask managers and peers about the organization's vision and their understanding of it.

Option 6: This option is correct. Collaborating with others outside your functional area or department can help you understand their points of view, get their support, and gain insight into how your decisions may affect them. This can help you develop a clear vision for your unit or department, and the role it should play in your organization as a whole.

BEING CREATIVE

Being creative

Another way to improve your ability to think strategically is to develop your creative thinking capacity. In combination with analysis, logic, and linear thinking, thinking creatively can offer a potentially comprehensive and practical approach to strategic thinking.

Creative thinking helps you avoid conformity, or reliance on what's simply accepted. You learn to develop and explore new ideas, and different ways of responding to and completing tasks. It also involves being open and ready to change your views about how things should work. This makes it easier to develop new processes or products, or better methods to serve customers.

To improve your ability to think creatively, you should cultivate two habits:
- challenge any assumptions you may have, and
- practice visualizing possibilities.

See each activity to learn more about it.

Challenge assumptions

Challenging assumptions involves challenging the way you and others think things should be done. This makes you more open-minded and better able to develop new ideas. For instance, you should ask yourself why a process is performed in a particular way and how else it could be done, instead of assuming there's no other way. This could help you improve the process or replace it with a better one.

It's also important to welcome provocative ideas instead of automatically resisting them. Even ideas that seem ridiculous at first may lead to innovative new ways of doing things once they're discussed and developed.

Practice visualizing

To teach yourself to think creatively, practice visualizing all the possibilities in a given situation. Regularly review what you think you know or the routine processes you use, and identify alternatives. This can help you become less rigid in your thinking and make it easier to identify opportunities and solutions to problems.

It may help to participate in a creative art form. For example, you might take painting or photography lessons. Participation in art forms like these, among others, exposes you to new patterns and may expand your perspective. During this process, keep track of how you're progressing and reacting, and make notes about what you observe about yourself and the situation you're in.

When you participate in a creative art form and record how you respond, you can develop strategic thinking skills because you get in the habit of changing your routine way of thinking.

In turn, this may improve the way you visualize and approach business issues.

Experiencing the arts can help strengthen mental agility and imagination as you seek parallels and patterns within a business context.

Being involved with the arts helps individuals to explore unknown territories in a manner that's perhaps different from the standard, linear way of thinking. It helps employees overcome uncertainties and take risks.

For this reason, many leading companies encourage employees to become involved with the arts so they can become more innovative and creative. They further encourage employees to see themselves as artists in the workplace. Work is a work of art that's being created for customers. The competitor becomes the teacher.

Question

What are some examples of ways to develop your creativity and therefore your ability to think strategically?

Options:

1. Talk to colleagues about ideas that initially seem too drastic or challenging

2. Sign up for guitar lessons at your local community center

3. Stick to one successful method of carrying out a task

4. Encourage employees to focus on making existing processes work

5. Identify as many different ways of achieving an objective as possible

Answer:

Option 1: This is a correct option. Thinking creatively involves challenging assumptions and being open to provocative ideas. This fuels innovation and makes it easier to think strategically.

Option 2: This option is correct. Becoming involved in different art forms helps to develop your creativity. Ideally you should take notes of your progress and experiences when trying out new art forms.

Option 3: This is an incorrect option. Being creative and thinking strategically is about having a broad perspective and being open to change, instead of relying on what has worked in the past. This often means reviewing familiar processes, and adapting or changing them to increase their success.

Option 4: This option is incorrect. To be creative and think strategically, you need to challenge assumptions about how things are done and be open to change and new ideas.

Option 5: This is a correct option. One way to develop your ability to think creatively is to practice visualizing the possibilities in any given situation, instead of accepting only one approach or "right" way of looking at things.

DEALING WITH COMPLEXITY

Dealing with complexity

To further develop your ability to think strategically, it's important to become accustomed to accepting and dealing with complexity. You need to get used to seeing things from a range of different perspectives and giving your attention to many things at once. To deal effectively with complexity, it helps to have a big picture view of your organization and know the importance of patterns and key causal relationships.

See each aspect of dealing with complexity to learn more about it.

Big picture view

You and your department function as part of a larger organization, and the organization itself functions in the context of a broad external environment. Thinking strategically means bearing this big picture view in mind when making decisions or taking actions. Your decisions and actions will affect not only your department, but your organization as a whole and its external environment.

So before overhauling a company web site, for example, an IT manager considers creating an online survey asking customers what changes they'd like to see. The manager also considers changing the company intranet, and meets with other departmental managers to get their views on how the intranet can be changed and how the changes will affect them.

Patterns and causal relationships

To develop effective strategic thinking skills, you need to recognize the relationships between different sections of your organization and understand their importance. Identifying patterns and trends in information or events can help you spot opportunities and develop solutions for addressing weaknesses.

For example, you need to consider customer complaints. You determine that, although complaints relate to different product features, the majority relate to the same component. Based on information in a company newsletter, you know your company obtains the component from a new spare parts supplier. By recognizing patterns and relationships, you've discovered the root cause of a large number of customer complaints. You can share this information with senior management and help address the issue.

As a functional manager, you need to ensure that your ideas align with strategic objectives.

Having a big picture view of your organization will help ensure you're familiar with its strategic vision and able to determine how this translates into particular objectives and goals for your department or business unit.

In turn, this will help ensure your decisions and actions help support your organization and align with its strategic direction.

Functional managers also have to balance the needs of various stakeholders.

This includes internal stakeholders such as employees, managers, and colleagues, as well as external stakeholders such as customers, shareholders, suppliers, creditors, and local communities.

Managers often have to balance the needs of customers and shareholders. For example, they strive to meet customers' needs – such as value for money, low prices, and high quality – at the same time as attempting to maximize shareholder wealth and company profitability. When these types of priorities conflict, managers have to make the best possible trade-offs.

Question

What are some ways you can deal with complexity and thereby improve your strategic thinking ability?

Options:

1. Think about your organization as part of a bigger system

2. Try to meet the needs of the most important stakeholders first

3. Try to recognize trends in information and events

4. Develop innovative ideas, regardless of whether they're aligned with your company's vision

Answer:

Option 1: This option is correct. Thinking strategically and dealing with complexities at different levels requires you to realize your department is part of a larger organization with its own external environment and specific strategic vision.

Option 2: This is an incorrect option. To deal with the complexities of different levels and views, it's important to balance the needs of numerous stakeholders, both internal and external.

Option 3: This is a correct option. To deal with complexity at different levels in a strategic manner, it's important to recognize patterns and trends in information or events. This makes it easier to develop solutions and make decisions.

Option 4: This option is incorrect. It's always important to ensure your ideas align with the strategic vision and objectives of your organization.

KNOWING WHAT'S GOING ON

Knowing what's going on

A final way to develop your strategic thinking ability is to make sure you know what's going on across your organization and its environment. This requires you look outside your department and assess both the organization's internal and external environments. Useful information you gather could relate to new ideas and trends, changes in customer needs, changes in competitive strategies, and internal challenges and changes.

You shouldn't limit yourself to specific sources of information. Instead, use a wide range of information sources. For instance, read industry journals, regularly visit relevant web sites, and scan news articles.

It can even be useful to review sources of information about companies or individuals who aren't in the same industry, but have different business perspectives that could spark new ideas for you.

It's essential to detect changes in the organization's environment because these changes may have significant effects both on the organization as a whole and on your business unit or department.

For instance, a book publisher who sells books through bookstores only notes a steady decrease in sales. He actively researches trends in the environment with the help of news articles and by visiting industry web sites. His research reveals that his company is failing to capitalize on the popularity of online book sales through popular web sites. This means the company is losing out on a big market of online buyers.

Constantly reviewing what's going on in different environments and collecting necessary information will help you build on your existing knowledge.

In this respect, avoid spending time trying to collect unnecessary information. Instead, seek to discover new information that can be used to further your strategy and that of your organization.

Use this information, combined with what you already know, to make innovative, effective decisions.

Question

What are some of the ways you can ensure you're aware of what's going on in your business environment?

Options:

1. Discuss changes in your business environment only with people in the same industry

2. Check out trends and ideas in industries outside your own

3. Review possible changes in customer needs on a regular basis

4. Rely on your experience in the organization to guide you

Answer:

Option 1: This is an incorrect option. Although it's important to speak to people who are in the same industry as you, you need to gather information from a wider range of sources. This could include reviewing the business perspectives of individuals in different industries.

Option 2: This option is correct. You can gather information about your business environment by collecting data relating to new ideas and trends from news articles. You can also find out how other industries are doing things – the ideas may apply to what you are doing too.

Option 3: This is a correct option. If you're aware of changes in the organization's external environment and in customers' needs, you're in a better position to respond to these changes.

Option 4: This option is incorrect. To be aware of what's going on in your business environment and what's changing, you have to build on existing knowledge by examining what's going on around you – inside and outside your organization.

DEVELOPING THE STRATEGIC THINKING SKILL OF SEEING THE BIG PICTURE

Developing the Strategic Thinking Skill of Seeing the Big Picture

People who think strategically in an organization constantly assess their broader environment. They consider industry and general economic trends, the organization's overall strategy, customers, and competition, and the challenges facing their own departments or business units. So they take a "big picture" view. Their awareness of the broad environment in which they're operating informs how they think, act, and make decisions.

The ideas and tools associated with systems thinking can help you uncover all your alternatives and gain a sense of the big picture. Systems thinking entails thinking of an organization as a large system, with its departments or divisions as various subsystems. In addition, the organization is part of a larger system, in the form of its business environment.

A key element of systems thinking is elevating your perspective so you can rise above your immediate circumstances. To do this, you need to identify where the boundaries are in your department and organization, and then look past those boundaries.

Boundaries may be clear physical boundaries such as office walls, or they may take more subtle forms such as traditional ways of doing things, assumptions about problems, and lack of information.

Needless to say, the world is often complex and confusing. To try to cope with this, people often ignore seeming contradictions or paradoxes. But a good way to practice systems thinking is to try to make sense out of opposites, contradictions, and paradoxes. To develop a systems thinking approach and thereby a big-picture view, you need to avoid reductionist thinking and explore more generative approaches.

Thinking strategically requires you to identify actions or decisions that will lead to success. Cause and effect relationships don't always apply. Given the many factors that may be involved, it can be difficult to come up with a simple cause and effect relationship. Systems thinkers focus instead on patterns and feedback loops, and constantly assess what is happening - rather than what should be happening. A reliance on what should be happening can lead to confirmation bias.

To think strategically and see the bigger picture, it's important to study both the external and internal contexts of your organization. This will help reveal the connections and interrelationships that exist. And you'll better understand your own role in the larger system and the impact of your decisions on other parts of the organization.

A useful tool for assessing the various external factors that affect organizations in your industry is Porter's model of five forces. Applying the model means you consider how your organization or department can respond to the forces of competition in a favorable manner. These forces are the bargaining power of customers and suppliers, the threat of new entrants into the market, the threat of substitutes, and rivalry among competitors.

Big-picture thinking isn't simply about being aware of external forces and how they interact with your organization. It's also about being aware of the internal context. You need to know how things work in your organization's particular corporate culture. You also need to establish how each function contributes to creating value for customers and supplying your organization's goods or services.

Strategic thinking requires that you recognize and address the concerns of internal stakeholders. What you do will impact others in your organization. Your decisions and actions may affect your supervisor, managers from other teams, and your reports.

To improve your big-picture thinking, it's useful to identify potential stakeholders, get information from these stakeholders, and look for additional ways to address their concerns.

By developing a systems-based perspective of your organization, you can gain a sense of the big picture needed in strategic thinking. This perspective enables you to create a mental model of the complete system of value creation within your organization. This model can highlight the interdependencies between functions and stakeholders, and help you to create and then supply value-added products and services to your customers.

You can gain a big-picture view of your organization and your role within it by mapping the organization's value chain. In addition, you can map its supply chain, which complements the value chain and refers to the flow of goods from suppliers to producers and then customers.

BIG-PICTURE THINKING

Big-picture thinking

People who think strategically in an organization constantly assess their broader environment. They consider industry and general economic trends, the organization's overall strategy, customers, and competition, and the challenges facing their own departments or business units. So they take a "big picture" view. Their awareness of the broad environment in which they're operating informs how they think, act, and make decisions.

Adopting a broad view can mean taking several steps:

- try to understand your organization's strategies and business environment,
- consider the impact of your decisions on the organization and other departments,
- identify the underlying reasons for your actions,
- consider how the parts of your organization interact, and
- develop a long-term vision.

Consider Maria, a design manager at an architectural firm. Over the past year, she's noticed a trend in clients requesting "green" architectural designs. She considers these in terms of the firm's strategic focus on producing innovative, high-quality buildings and structures. Maria does some research into biomimicry to find out what new products are available and what designs her team could produce using nature as inspiration.

When Maria is asked to submit a design for a bid to construct an office building in a warm country, she decides to use building materials that reduce the carbon footprint. She works on designs that use extremely energy-efficient cooling techniques – modeled on those used in nature by termites and cacti.

She does an impact analysis of the cost, quality, and construction time with the new material and designs from the perspective of customer and supplier. During the early prototype stage, she speaks to key suppliers to check the availability and price of the material.

Maria's company wins the bid and constructs the office building. A few months after the client moves into the new building, Maria gets feedback from the client about the design and material. Responses are favorable and the building wins various awards for the firm.

Maria's able to anticipate opportunities in terms of green products and designs. She's also able to link her decisions with the organization's strategic direction and overall business goals.

She realizes how her decisions can impact customers and others outside the organization. She also contributes to the organization's business goals of producing innovative, high-quality buildings and structures.

Taking a broad perspective is an important aspect of thinking strategically and can have several benefits. It helps you to anticipate internal and external opportunities and challenges. You learn to understand your organization's strategic direction better, so you can make decisions that align with organizational goals. Taking a big-picture view can also help you understand your role and contributions in relation to your organization's goals. Finally, you can realize the impact of your work on stakeholders in and outside the organization.

SYSTEMS THINKING

Systems thinking

The ideas and tools associated with systems thinking can help you uncover all your alternatives and gain a sense of the big picture. Systems thinking entails thinking of an organization as a large system, with its departments or divisions as various subsystems.

In addition, the organization is part of a larger system, in the form of its business environment.

Systems thinking requires you take on a holistic view of your organization and situations you have to deal with. So you need to consider how each system works and how subsystems are interconnected. To do this, you need to understand your actions and decisions in the larger context, while also being able to focus on details.

See each element of systems thinking for more information about it.

Holistic

With systems thinking, you need to see as much of the system as possible – what your department is working toward, what your entire organization is working toward, and the industry context that your organization works within.

This way of thinking can prevent people from shifting problems elsewhere or creating new problems as a result of narrow or "quick fix" decisions.

Interconnected

What happens in organizations, like in systems, is complex. A change made in one area affects other areas, sometimes in unpredictable ways.

By recognizing that each part or subsystem is interconnected and interdependent, you can better determine the potential effects of change – not only within your department, but in other departments too.

In context

Systems thinking depends on the ability to focus on your organization's vision, at the same time as keeping a detailed view of your own department's role, challenges, and goals in mind. Being able to switch perspectives, or even to hold both perspectives in your mind at the same time, takes time and practice but brings positive results.

Focusing on the right level of detail is as important as viewing the organization as a whole and with a long-term view.

Contextual thinking shifts managers' perspectives between detail and broad overviews. Suppose an operations manager at an airliner leads a team at a busy airport. Considering the shrinking market share, fierce competition, and high fixed costs, the company's strategic vision centers around an exemplary customer service and achieving the highest level of customer satisfaction.

However, one of the manager's key goals is customer safety and cooperating with airport security agencies.

Often the two goals conflict and sometimes a security measure will cause customer dissatisfaction.

The manager understands that the two goals need to be balanced. Her strategy is to compensate for the customer dissatisfaction where she can – by offering gifts, and quick and courteous customer service at counters. She also aims to restore customer confidence and satisfaction by communicating the need for security measures.

Adopting systems thinking will improve decision making because it gives you a better understanding of the complexity of the problems your decisions aim to solve. It also provides a structured way to balance a broad perspective with the ability to take the details into account.

See each benefit of systems thinking for more information about it.

Improve decision making

Using systems thinking helps prevent people from attempting to apply short-term solutions to long-term problems.

Knowing that problems don't exist in isolation helps you to solve those problems completely, without overlooking aspects of the problems in linked areas or accidentally giving rise to new problems. So solutions are more far reaching and better address both the roots of the problems and the various effects.

Balance broad perspective with details

Systems thinking requires attention to detail as well as a broad and complete view of your organization. Through big-picture thinking and analysis, you develop a structured way of balancing these two perspectives. The guidelines for strategic thinking provide the structure for shifting from a details view to a broad view and back again.

As a result, you learn how to balance the urgent issues in your department against the issues that are important to your organization. This means solutions you develop have a longer-term positive effect.

Often making short-sighted changes to parts of a natural ecosystem results in unwanted effects elsewhere in the system. For example, introducing a fast-growing, non-indigenous shrub in order to stabilize sand dunes could result in the shrub crowding out, and eventually killing, other indigenous plants. Those plants might be the only food source for a particular animal.

Similar chains of cause and effect often apply in business. With systems thinking, you can avoid the types of poor judgment that may result from focusing too narrowly on just one business area, or just one aspect of a problem.

The ideas of systems thinking that can help you gain a sense of the big picture include elevating your perspective, understanding paradoxes, and understanding causality.

ELEVATING PERSPECTIVE

Elevating perspective

A key element of systems thinking is elevating your perspective so you can rise above your immediate circumstances. To do this, you need to identify where the boundaries are in your department and organization, and then look past those boundaries.

Boundaries may be clear physical boundaries such as office walls, or they may take more subtle forms such as traditional ways of doing things, assumptions about problems, and lack of information.

Looking past boundaries may be as simple as taking your first tour around your whole organization or setting up regular cross-departmental meetings to share information.

However, what's really needed is a shift in perspective – in how you view your work and your organization.

To broaden your perspective and enable you to look past boundaries, you can use two main strategies – develop a reflective approach to your actions and decisions, and look for similarities amid the differences.

See each strategy for more information.

Develop a reflective approach

A fair amount of managerial or supervisory work is routine – once you're used to it, you can do it with little or no critical thought. Generally, it's only when something unexpected happens or you're faced with uncertainty that you're prompted to explore your understanding of how things are or how they work.

To broaden your perspective, aim to think critically more often, reflecting on and questioning what you know, what your role is, and what impact you can have.

Look for similarities

People naturally look for and notice differences. When you begin to look for similarities in seemingly different things, it often results in a change of perspective and enables you to look past boundaries.

You should practice seeking out similarities among different companies, internal departments, people, situations, and problems you encounter.

For example, lean philosophy was developed and implemented in the Japanese motor industry. It's tenets and practices were then adopted by industries as diverse as health care and financial services, providing dramatic and tangible results.

Question

How can you elevate your perspective and thereby gain a sense of the bigger picture?

Options:

1. Identify physical and mental boundaries in your department

2. Aim to question what you know, your role, and what impact you have regularly

3. Look for differences between your department and others

4. Select one strategy and then find as many justifications for it as possible

Answer:

Option 1: This is a correct option. You need to identify where the boundaries are in your department and organization, and then look past those boundaries.

Option 2: This option is correct. You gain a sense of the bigger picture by developing a reflective approach, where you question yourself about what you do, what you know, and how your actions impact others.

Option 3: This is an incorrect option. People have a natural tendency to look for differences. When you look for similarities instead, you are more likely to view things in a new light and elevate your perspective.

Option 4: This option is incorrect. Elevating your perspective is about identifying boundaries and moving past them. This includes developing a reflective approach and looking for similarities that could remove boundaries.

UNDERSTANDING PARADOXES

Understanding paradoxes

Needless to say, the world is often complex and confusing. To try to cope with this, people often ignore seeming contradictions or paradoxes. But a good way to practice systems thinking is to try to make sense out of opposites, contradictions, and paradoxes. To develop a systems thinking approach and thereby a big-picture view, you need to avoid reductionist thinking and explore more generative approaches.

See each strategy for more information about it.

Avoid reductionist thinking

A reductionist approach involves breaking down information, eliminating anything that's judged invalid or contradictory, in an attempt to uncover a single, unquestionable truth. Both in science and business, this approach ignores complexity and the importance of context.

As an example, a manager tries to reduce a problem involving low productivity to a single cause, like a flawed departmental process or unmotivated employees.

Explore generative approaches

In a generative approach, you consider what you can add rather than what you can remove from the information at hand. You branch out from one idea or issue to others, and make connections.

For example, a manager associates a problem involving low productivity with a range of other problems, like ineffective human resources management and poor communication among different departments.

So generative thinking requires you to make connections where seemingly there are none. You do this with the intention of identifying new possibilities.

Sometimes making links means considering seemingly ridiculous possibilities. For example, a pizza manufacturer expands its product offering by creating a successful promotional run of pizza-flavored ice cream.

It can help to collaborate with and understand other parts of your organization. Then you'll be able to understand the reason behind a seemingly contradictory action – you'll understand the perspective and thinking behind that action.

To understand and work with paradoxes, you need to find ways of becoming comfortable with tensions involved in dealing with complex circumstances. To do this, you need to draw on conscious analysis, as well as intuition to create order and make sense of situations. This can be a collective activity, involving interaction among individuals in the organization.

Question

Which examples illustrate how you can make sense out of opposites, contradictions, and paradoxes, which will help you to gain a sense of the big picture?

Options:

1. When examining two seemingly opposing ideas, you imagine the possibilities of each and the viewpoints that led to both

2. You meet with managers from other departments to find out why they took a certain action

3. You make sense of contradictions by making sure your viewpoint is communicated the most persuasively

4. You focus on reducing several opposing ideas to the single best one

Answer:

Option 1: This option is correct. Instead of looking for a single and best possible idea, you use a process that is adaptive and generative. You're open to contradictions, suspending judgment and inviting new possibilities by thinking about the viewpoints behind the ideas.

Option 2: This is a correct option. Collaboration and insight from different areas can help you understand contradictions and paradoxes you may encounter. This also gives you a broader picture of the organization.

Option 3: This option is incorrect. To think strategically, you need to be open to contradictions, rather than focus on how to make your own viewpoint persuasive.

Option 4: This is an incorrect option. Eliminating opposing ideas to find a single, best idea is not a characteristic of strategic thinking. When you're thinking strategically, you embrace opposing ideas. You work to expand on them so you can generate ideas and possibilities from each.

UNDERSTANDING CAUSALITY

Understanding causality

Thinking strategically requires you to identify actions or decisions that will lead to success. Cause and effect relationships don't always apply. Given the many factors that may be involved, it can be difficult to come up with a simple cause and effect relationship. Systems thinkers focus instead on patterns and feedback loops, and constantly assess what is happening - rather than what should be happening. A reliance on what should be happening can lead to confirmation bias.

Confirmation bias happens when you look for information that will validate your beliefs. This often happens because it's easier to confirm an idea than spend energy on challenging it and coming up with something new. The danger of confirmation bias is that you could miss critical information.

You can counter the tendency toward confirmation bias by using hypothesis testing.

Using hypothesis testing, you begin by asking a "what if" question such as "What if flexible working hours increased productivity?"

You follow this with a series of "if ... then" hypotheses. For example, you might state "If employees have more flexible working hours, productivity should improve." Then you might state "If flexible working hours negatively affect productivity, allowing flextime will reduce productivity."

You then evaluate the data at your disposal to determine whether providing flextime actually has a positive or negative effect on productivity. You can come up with a variety of hypotheses, without sacrificing the ability to explore new ideas and approaches. Hypothesis testing helps you go beyond simplistic notions of cause and effect, and improves and expands thinking.

You can also use a basic influence diagram to understand the multidirectional nature of the cause and effect different variables have on a decision and how they interact to influence it. In this type of diagram, the issue under consideration is displayed in a rectangle, and the variables are the ovals.

All the elements are linked by directional arrows which indicate their direction of influence. Plus or minus signs indicate an increase or a decrease in the value of the influence. And where the influential effect between elements is delayed, two parallel lines break the directional flow between them.

Question

What examples illustrate the use of the systems view of cause and effect, which can help you gain a sense of the big picture in your organization?

Options:

1. Consider long-term patterns and feedback on what is happening

2. Propose different "what if" scenarios to explore causal relationships

3. Create a diagram that maps influences on different factors

4. Confirm your assumptions before you begin looking for new causes

5. For each factor that has led to success, determine its one cause

Answer:

Option 1: This option is correct. Systems thinkers focus instead on patterns and feedback loops, and constantly assess what is happening - rather than what should be happening.

Option 2: This is a correct option. Exploring "what if" scenarios is an aspect of hypothesis testing, which helps you go beyond simplistic linear notions of cause and effect and improves and expands thinking.

Option 3: This option is correct. A basic influence diagram helps you to understand how different elements interact and the multidirectional nature of cause and effect.

Option 4: This is an incorrect option. Confirming your assumptions is an example of confirmation bias, which involves accepting only information that validates what you already believe. This type of bias discourages systems thinking.

Option 5: This option is incorrect. Multiple factors may influence an outcome. Systems thinking helps you to expand notions of causality rather than reducing events to a single cause.

UNDERSTANDING CONTEXTS

Understanding contexts

To think strategically and see the bigger picture, it's important to study both the external and internal contexts of your organization. This will help reveal the connections and interrelationships that exist. And you'll better understand your own role in the larger system and the impact of your decisions on other parts of the organization.

To begin understanding the broader context in which you operate, you should consider the relationships among the corporate, business, and functional levels of your organization. You also need to pay attention to how your strategies and decisions may impact the organization, its stakeholders, and its external environment.

Strategic thinkers are constantly aware of various forces that shape the industry they're in and its competitive environment. Translating this into effective management, strategic thinkers balance these factors and make decisions that take them into account.

Question

How would you rate your current awareness of your organization's external context?

Options:

1. Very good
2. Moderate
3. Poor

Answer:

Option 1: You say your current awareness is very good. Being aware of your organization's external context is an important ability to have as a strategic thinker, and this course will help you to develop that ability further. You can practice and hone your skills and awareness, looking at both external and internal contexts to develop a big-picture view.

Option 2: You say your current awareness is moderate. This course will provide you with the tools to help you increase that awareness and prepare you for more in-depth strategic thinking.

Option 3: You say your current awareness is poor. To become a strategic thinker, you need to equip yourself with the tools that enable you to increase your awareness and practice more strategic thinking in your work. This course will help you do this.

PORTER'S FIVE FORCES

Porter's five forces

A useful tool for assessing the various external factors that affect organizations in your industry is Porter's model of five forces. Applying the model means you consider how your organization or department can respond to the forces of competition in a favorable manner. These forces are the bargaining power of customers and suppliers, the threat of new entrants into the market, the threat of substitutes, and rivalry among competitors.

See each competitive force to find out more about it.

Bargaining power of customers

Customers influence profitability by using their buying power to demand low prices and expensive product specifications. They may also play competitors against each other to get what they want.

Customers are the most powerful when economies of scale are important and the customers are in a position to make large-volume purchases. Customers can also be a threat if they have the potential to integrate backward –

for example producing their own components instead of purchasing them.

Bargaining power of suppliers

Suppliers exert force if an industry is dominated by only a few suppliers, if the supplied product or material is rare or unique, or if suppliers determine that industries other than yours are a higher priority.

Organizations may be forced to deal with slim profit margins because of high production costs or production delays because of their inability to obtain or afford input materials or services. Suppliers can also be a threat if they have the potential to integrate forward – producing the same products and services, thereby becoming your competitors.

Threat of new entrants

New entrants are organizations entering a market for the first time. They increase the intensity of competition, forcing prices and profits down.

New entrants may also have innovative advantages such as proprietary knowledge and patents that make their products attractive and outdate competing products.

Threat of substitutes

Substitutes are goods and services that consumers perceive to be reasonably interchangeable.

The threat of substitutes is highest when customers and end users can easily switch to buying alternative products instead of buying yours.

Rivalry among competitors

Rivalry, or competition, forces organizations to work with lower profit margins or risk losing sales completely. When rivalry is strong, organizations typically go into defensive mode, diverting focus and resources away from innovation and long-term, value-adding activities.

Rivalry is a significant force when competitors are matched in size and economic strength, the pool of competitors is large, sales growth is slow or historically steady, there is little product differentiation, or competitors have similar marketing strategies.

Using Porter's model, you can take three steps to develop a big-picture view of the external forces affecting your organization and become a better strategic thinker. First determine key players in each category. Then analyze the various forces in more depth. And finally, devise strategies that take the relevant external forces into account.

To begin, you identify the key players involved in each of the five categories of external forces. For example, who are your organization's main suppliers, and which suppliers have the power to significantly affect your costs?

Once you're clear who the key players are, you analyze each external factor in more depth. For example, if you want to further your knowledge of customers, you can ask questions such as "Is the market dominated by a few large-volume buyers?" "How price-sensitive are customers?" and "How important is the product to customers?"

As a final step, you need to devise appropriate strategies using the information about your organization's external context. For example, an analysis of competitive forces can help a departmental manager determine a purchase strategy, set prices, devise competitive marketing campaigns, and decide on product design and features.

Sorin Dumitrascu

A general manager of a hotel chain decides to think about ways to boost profitability. She wants to determine the hotel's key players and then analyze the five forces – the bargaining power of customers and suppliers, the threat of new entrants and substitutes, and the hotel's rivals.

See each factor for details of how the hotel manager identifies key players and analyzes the forces.

Customers

The hotel manager notes that key customers are events organizers and large corporations with steady requirements for hotel services.

She also notes that a high volume of independent visitors to her city are business travelers.

Suppliers

The manager determines that providers of cleaning, gardening, and laundry services are the hotel's biggest suppliers.

Also, the hotel depends heavily on daily supplies of fresh produce for its restaurant. The current supplier has the largest market share and provides the freshest produce. However, despite being a large supplier, its prices are always above market level. Few other suppliers are willing to meet the comparatively small daily orders at reasonable prices, preferring to provide larger orders directly to supermarket chains.

New entrants

The hotel manager asks questions like, "Do existing competitors have a cost advantage over new entrants?" "How will brand loyalty affect new entrants?" and "What control do existing players have over access to raw materials and distribution channels?"

In this case, the manager rates the threat of new entrants as moderate because the capital costs of entering the hotel market are high. Existing key players' access to raw materials and control of distribution channels are also barriers for new entrants to the local hotel industry.

Substitutes

Questions the hotel manager should ask when analyzing substitutes include, "Can customers switch products easily?" and "How viable and valuable are substitute products?"

The hotel manager identifies three large hotels in the area as substitutes because they attract a large share of the business traveler market. Also, hotel customers who become dissatisfied with her hotel's services could move to one of the substitute hotels, which provides spas and other luxury features associated with five-star accommodation.

Rivals

Strategies that are effective against new entrants to the market may be ineffective against existing competitors. Established companies have advantages such as widespread brand recognition, exclusive deals with customers and suppliers, or proprietary elements – such as copyrights, patents, or trade secrets – that can't be duplicated or imittated.

The hotel manager identifies the other three hotels, that are part of large chains, as her hotel's main rivals. As the industry becomes more competitive, hotel chains compete for customers at the national level.

As a final step, the hotel manager devises different strategies for increasing the hotel's profitability. For example, she negotiates lower prices with two other suppliers of farm produce to reduce the hotel's reliance on one supplier.

Because business travelers are the most powerful customers, she wants to offer them special discounts and loyalty programs to win their repeat business.

She knows advertising needs to change to attract other customer segments and reduce the power business travelers currently hold.

Question

In considering the broader organizational context, a marketing manager at an athletic shoe manufacturer realizes his company is facing high levels of competition and substitution due to low-price imports. He also discovers the majority of customers are in their mid-twenties, and they are concerned with style and celebrities.

Which approaches take the external factors into account and so illustrate the use of big-picture thinking?

Options:

1. Consider basing the company's competitive strategy on product styling and endorsements from popular sports figures

2. Think of possible ways the organization might reduce costs and pass those on in the form of reduced prices

3. Refocus marketing on an older group of customers who can afford higher prices

4. Stick to what the organization has done in the past to succeed to define what it should do now

Answer:

Option 1: This is the correct option. By focusing on a niche area, the marketing manager shows big- picture thinking in response to customer analysis.

Option 2: This option is correct. This approach takes into account the external factor of substitute products.

Option 3: This option is incorrect. This would entail a shift to a completely new customer base, when in fact an existing customer base can be tapped if its needs are properly met.

Option 4: This is an incorrect option. Taking a broader view means looking at the external context and thinking about how to incorporate it into your strategic thinking.

UNDERSTANDING INTERNAL DIRECTION

Understanding internal direction

Big-picture thinking isn't simply about being aware of external forces and how they interact with your organization. It's also about being aware of the internal context. You need to know how things work in your organization's particular corporate culture. You also need to establish how each function contributes to creating value for customers and supplying your organization's goods or services.

A key element of strategic thinking is aligning what you do with your organization's vision and strategic direction. If each part of an organization moves in the same direction, the organization's vision is much more likely to become a reality.

As a department or functional manager, you use strategic thinking to determine how to meet your department's goals and, at the same time, support your organization's vision. For example, if your organization's vision includes achieving efficient and eco-friendly production, you might consider reducing your department's use of materials and focus on implementing efficient processes that minimize wastes harmful to the environment.

To align your department's goals with your organization's vision and strategic plans, you can follow specific steps:

1. find out what your organization's strategic plans are,

2. talk with others to deepen your understanding of organizational strategies,

3. consider the goals for your department that will contribute to the success of organizational strategies, and

4. consider how to balance short-term requirements with long-term goals.

See each step for examples of how to align your department's goals with your organization's vision and strategic plans.

1. Find strategic plans

You can find out whether your organization has strategic plans by asking your supervisor, reviewing planning documentation, reading company reports and the company's web site, and tracking the organization's investments.

These can all provide valuable information about what's important for your organization and what direction it's heading in.

2. Talk with others

To gain a deeper understanding of your organization's vision and your department's role in this vision, it's helpful to talk with other managers in your organization.

You can deepen your understanding by finding out what they're doing to achieve strategic goals and to answer their questions around what your department is or could be doing.

3. Consider goals

As your understanding of organizational strategy deepens, you can assess what goals your department could set that would bring the organization closer to achieving its strategic goals.

Note what plans you already have and ask yourself whether these advance or form barriers to the organization's overall strategy.

4. Balance requirements with goals

Because strategic thinking and a big-picture view require that you consider both short-term and long-term requirements and goals, it's important to determine how best to balance these two.

Discuss with your boss what weight to give to short-term and long-term requirements. Then keep a log and review how well your department is able to keep this balance. Check in with your team members for their ideas on how to create this balance too.

Question

A production manager for a furniture manufacturer understands that the company's vision is to produce high-quality products using environmentally sustainable methods. However, he wants to get a broader picture of the organization's direction.

What steps can he take to do this?

Options:

1. Note on the company web site that the organization plans to reduce waste by 20% and increase reliance on renewable materials

2. Reflect on the news that the organization has invested in a sustainable logging enterprise

3. Consider that other managers are focusing on streamlining their processes and working to incorporate green practices

4. Note what strategic goals rival organizations have adopted in the past

5. Consider the impact new entrants may have on organizational profits

Answer:

Option 1: This is a correct option. Speaking with your boss, and reading the company web site or planning documents, can help you gain a broader picture of your organization's strategic direction.

Option 2: This option is correct. Noting how your organization allocates its resources can help you gain a deeper sense of its strategic direction and goals.

Option 3: This is a correct option. Speaking with colleagues helps you gain a broader sense of how your decisions and plans could support organizational goals and other departments.

Option 4: This option is incorrect. In this scenario, you need to explore internal factors. Find out what the organization is doing and what its people are saying to help determine its strategic direction, and determine how best you can align with this.

Option 5: This option is incorrect. This focus is an external one. The scenario calls for an internal review of what the organization is doing to move toward its strategic goals.

CONSIDERING STAKEHOLDERS

Considering stakeholders

Strategic thinking requires that you recognize and address the concerns of internal stakeholders. What you do will impact others in your organization. Your decisions and actions may affect your supervisor, managers from other teams, and your reports.

To improve your big-picture thinking, it's useful to identify potential stakeholders, get information from these stakeholders, and look for additional ways to address their concerns.

See each step for an example of what it involves.

Identify potential stakeholders

Use brainstorming to generate a list of people who may be affected by your decisions or who may have an interest in the outcomes of what you do. Consider what their roles and goals are, and what responsibilities and relationships they have.

For example, a design manager may view manufacturing, marketing, suppliers, and customers as key stakeholders.

Get information

Where possible, gather information directly from stakeholders by letting them know what your ideas are and asking them for their feedback. In particular, ask questions about what problems they foresee and what solutions they can identify.

For example, you might ask stakeholders from the Manufacturing Department about any problems they foresee in manufacturing bamboo instead of hardwood furniture.

Address concerns

When discussing your intentions with stakeholders, keep an open mind and listen to their concerns and ideas. This will enable you to keep searching for additional ways to solve problems and to align your work with organizational goals.

When thinking about a strategic direction, you may be tempted to choose an option from the first few alternatives that arise, but try to resist doing this.

Instead, allow the list of possibilities to grow significantly before you make a choice.

Suppose a manager is thinking about adopting a new database to manage supplier relationships. This idea may raise concerns for the IT Department, which would need to install and manage the database. The Finance Department may be worried about the cost of the new software. Managers from other departments may not want to make the shift and your employees will have to learn how to use the new system. These are all stakeholder concerns you should take into account.

Question

Consider the manager at the furniture manufacturer. Thinking about the organization's overall direction has led him to consider the goal of introducing a quality audit process in his department. He now wants to consider what this might mean for relevant stakeholders.

What should he do?

Options:

1. List other potential goals that may accommodate stakeholders' needs better

2. Create a full list of those who could be affected by the decision

3. Speak to his employees and supervisor about the idea

4. Try out the plan over a single month and find out who the change affected and in what ways

5. Review whether his plan aligns with other companies' approaches in different industries

Answer:

Option 1: This is a correct option. You should avoid the temptation to go with the first few options that arise. Instead expand on the possible ways you can deal with an issue.

Option 2: This option is correct. It's important to identify all stakeholders so you can take their concerns into account.

Option 3: This is a correct option. Stakeholders who are likely to be affected by the manager's idea are employees, and his supervisor. For example, how the audit will affect productivity and how the results will be used.

Option 4: This is an incorrect option. It's important to discuss issues and potential problems with stakeholders.

Trying things out without having this discussion is likely to build resentment and may waste time and resources.

Option 5: This option is incorrect. The manager needs to identify internal stakeholders, gather more information from them, and generate more ideas through this discussion. It isn't necessary at this point to consider external forces.

VALUE AND VALUE CHAINS

Value and value chains

By developing a systems-based perspective of your organization, you can gain a sense of the big picture needed in strategic thinking. This perspective enables you to create a mental model of the complete system of value creation within your organization. This model can highlight the interdependencies between functions and stakeholders, and help you to create and then supply value-added products and services to your customers.

To apply the model, you need to understand how value is defined in business and what your business's value chain consists of.

See each concept to find out more about it.

Value

Value in this context is anything your organization provides that customers are willing to pay for. For instance, value may be added through the basic design of a product that's useful to customers, safety features on a vehicle, after-sales support for a software program, or tax services at an accountancy firm.

Value chain

A value chain is the sequence of activities or events through which an organization creates and delivers value for its customers. It consists of interdependent processes that work together to generate value, and the resulting demand and cash flow this creates.

Porter identifies nine generic value-added activities that may be included in an organization's value chain. Five of the nine categories are value-adding, or primary, activities essential for an organization's operations. These are directly related to the creation of products and services:

- inbound logistics – activities concerned with receiving and storing raw materials, input services, and making them available to operations,
- operations – activities associated with transforming input materials and services into finished products and services,
- outbound logistics – activities associated with collecting, warehousing, and distributing finished products and services,
- marketing and sales – activities associated with identifying customer needs, and generating and making sales, and
- service – activities associated with supporting the product or service after it is sold to the customer.

The remaining four categories of value-added activities support the primary activities, as well as ongoing operations. They don't directly add value, but operations are not possible without them. Porter classifies support activities as follows:

- infrastructure – activities associated with general management, planning, finance, accounting, government affairs, and quality management
- human resource management – activities involved with employee recruitment, hiring, training, development, and compensation
- technology development – activities that support or improve the product or associated processes, and procurement – activities related to purchasing raw materials, supplies, and equipment.

Question

Match each activity category to the corresponding activity type. More than one category may match to an activity type.

Options:

A. Inbound logistics

B. Procurement

C. Service

D. Infrastructure

Targets:

1. Primary activity

2. Support activity

Answer:

Primary activities, which produce what customers are willing to pay for, include inbound logistics, operations, outbound logistics, marketing and sales, and service.

Support activities support primary value-adding activities or ongoing operations. They include procurement, infrastructure, human resource management, and technology development.

SUPPLY AND VALUE CHAINS

Supply and value chains

You can gain a big-picture view of your organization and your role within it by mapping the organization's value chain. In addition, you can map its supply chain, which complements the value chain and refers to the flow of goods from suppliers to producers and then customers.

See each type of chain for more information about how mapping it can help you develop a big-picture view.

Value chain

If you understand how and where your organization is succeeding in creating value for customers, you can focus on prioritizing these areas. Understanding the organization's value chain will also make it clear how the different parts of your organization, together with external parties like suppliers, play a role in how value is created and delivered to the customer.

For example, examining a value chain may make it clear how a department that designs interfaces for software depends on other departments, including those that market, test, package, and distribute the software. So it can place the focus on working together to achieve common goals, rather than on each department's goals in isolation.

Supply chain

A supply chain focuses on costs and efficiencies in material flows as the product moves toward completion. By approaching production from this perspective, you are better able to spot ways of improving efficiency and reducing waste.

Examining an overall supply chain also identifies all the internal and external parties involved in delivering a product to customers. So it focuses attention on the supply system as a whole, rather than on individual parts of it, or departments.

By integrating the value chain and the supply chain, you gain a comprehensive view of what an organization does, the order it does it in, and the organization's key components or functions. You get an overview of how raw material, input services, and information flow to create products and services. Value chains, in particular, map out the activities an organization undertakes to create value and gain a competitive advantage.

Visual representations of value and supply chains can help give you a holistic view of the organization because you see how your own work contributes to creating value for customers and other stakeholders.

If you have a good understanding of value and supply chains, you can better understand the organization's strategic focus and how it connects to the activities of each department. This makes it easier to align with the organization's strategy.

To think strategically, you keep this holistic view in mind when making your own day-to-day decisions.

A value chain helps you see which activities have the most potential to add value. You can then prioritize work according to how it affects primary activities, thereby helping your organization obtain a competitive advantage. For example, it may be appropriate to prioritize activities related to operations or service, or activities related to the connections between different parts of the chain.

See each potential area of focus for an example of how competitive advantage can be sought as a result of value chain analysis.

Operations

A bearings manufacturer's organizational strategy focuses on high quality and efficiency in its operations. After studying operations, the plant manager at one of its production units identifies preventive maintenance as a key activity for gaining competitive advantage. He suspects that increasing the frequency of machine maintenance will result in far less defects, rework, and scrap being generated in the company's operations.

Although preventive maintenance is expensive, the added costs are offset by a reduced need for quality control. So the manager uses the value chain analysis to recognize opportunities to create value and achieve organizational goals.

Service

The management team at an online bank identifies the service its help desk provides as an activity critical to its organizational goal of delivering superior customer support. Management decides to differentiate its organization's help desk from competitors' by adding value to this activity.

The company refocuses its help desk operators' training to customer satisfaction, making sure that operators are trained in handling all types of customer requests and complaints.

Connections

A manufacturing company's value chain is nearly identical to that of its rivals, so the operations manager examines links between activities as a source of competitive advantage. This calls for a seamless coordination among various departments where they hand over information and work-in-progress to the next stage in the value chain.

For example, the Marketing and Sales Departments must deliver sales forecasts to the Procurement and Operations departments accurately and on time. This information helps Procurement order the required materials by the right dates. Operations is able to do production planning. Procurement must deliver order information to Inbound Logistics in a timely fashion so that Operations can schedule production and deliver products as scheduled by the Marketing and Sales Departments.

Question

How can assessing value and supply chains help give you a big-picture view of your organization and your role in it?

Options:

1. You can gain an overview of the entire organization and what goes into creating a single product or service

2. You can develop a better sense of where your division adds value for the customer or supports processes that add value

3. You gain a sense of the organization's values and strategies, and are better able to implement them

4. You have greater awareness of how your decisions affect those both upstream and downstream in the process

5. You can focus on your area of expertise and ensure processes within your division operate smoothly

6. You gain competitive advantage by noting links between divisions

Answer:

Option 1: This is a correct option. Value chains and supply chains trace processes and activities across different organizational functions and divisions. This enables you to understand how the parts of the organization interact to create products or services that customers value, and what your role is in that.

Option 2: This option is correct. Value chains highlight the activities that directly add value to your company's goods or services and the activities that support those processes. They make it clear how different organizational functions are interconnected.

Option 3: This is a correct option. A value chain provides an overview of how an organization provides value, or what a customer is prepared to pay for. A supply chain outlines the flow of materials from suppliers through to an end product. By reviewing these chains, you gain a deeper understanding of how the parts of an organization work together to achieve common goals, which in turn guides your thinking about how to help implement organizational strategies.

Option 4: This option is correct. Value and supply chains outline what occurs both before and after a department you manage plays its part in overall production. Knowing what is upstream or downstream from your area can help you understand the impact of your actions and decisions.

Option 5: This is an incorrect option. Value and supply chains provide a broad view of an entire process across divisions within an organization. These tools don't focus on specific functions or areas of expertise.

Option 6: This option is incorrect. In some cases, you can optimize activities that relate to connections between departments, or between production and service provision. However, each organization needs to find sources for possible competitive advantage. This won't always relate to links between business divisions or functions.

THE SIPOC DIAGRAM

The SIPOC diagram

To further help with thinking strategically by having a big-picture view, you can use a SIPOC diagram. SIPOC stands for Suppliers, Inputs, Process, Outputs, and Customers. The purpose of the diagram is to show how inputs and outputs flow from suppliers to customers. You read a SIPOC diagram from left to right. Suppliers and their inputs are displayed on the left. In the center are the high-level steps of the process. Outputs and customers are listed on the right.

Suppliers

Suppliers provide the inputs, or resources and information, for the process. In the car repair example, suppliers include the auto parts distributor and car owner.

Inputs

Inputs are the resources and information the suppliers provide. The process uses the inputs to produce outputs. In the car repair example, the inputs are the auto parts and the car.

Process

The process is the series of steps that converts the inputs into outputs. In the car repair example, the process includes steps a car owner and a mechanic must perform.

The Process column states "Process description: repair of car damaged in a collision." It also contains a process map detailing the following steps: customer drops off car, assign mechanic to inspect car, estimate repair cost and time, get customer insurance approval, order and install parts, test drive, and customer picks up car. These steps are placed in rectangular shapes and are connected with directional arrows.

Outputs

Outputs are the products or services produced by the process. The output of the car repair process, for example, is a repaired car.

Customers

Customers are the individuals and organizations that receive the outputs of a process. The customers of the car repair process are the car's owner and, when relevant, the insurance company involved in paying for repairs.

A detailed visual presentation like the SIPOC diagram, as well as diagrams of the value and supply chains, help you develop big-picture thinking by providing a high-level map and linear description. They show connections between processes, and between internal and external stakeholders, and what key inputs and dependencies exist.

See each way that a high-level diagram supports strategic thinking for an example of it.

High-level map

Both a SIPOC diagram and a value or supply chain provide a high-level view of what an organization and its various departments do to create and deliver a product, a service, or value for its customers. A high-level view allows managers to see the impact of a departmental decision or activity on other departments and the entire organization strategically.

For example, a call center manager for software support may view the entire process for creating the software. She sees how the software was tested, how the specifications were gathered, and why her support adds value to the product. She'll then know how making changes in one activity – for example software specifications – may affect the outcome in other departments and also in the achievement of the organization's strategic goals.

Linear process

Visual overview maps such as the SIPOC diagram and the value chain provide a linear description of how different processes are connected throughout an entire organization.

For example, a map may outline the purchase of components, the delivery of components to storage areas, the production of a product, and its storage, transport, and sale.

Connections

High-level diagrams outline how various internal and external stakeholders are connected to each other. For example, suppliers and purchasers are directly connected. They are indirectly connected to marketers, sales personnel, producers, and customers.

By viewing the entire process for creating a product or service, you establish how different departments rely on one another and interact to create the product or service.

Inputs and dependencies

High-level diagrams summarize information – they tend to show only the key inputs and outputs within a process. For example, in a map of the movement from specifications to design of a software program, a key input may be customer requirements and the key output is the approved design.

Dependencies between divisions and processes are also covered, however. For example, the Sales Department may have to determine the customer specifications, whereas the Software Development Department has to sign off on the design.

Question

Which examples illustrate how an understanding of the organizational value chain can help you see the big picture?

Options:

1. A finance manager understands he should prioritize funding for primary activities

2. A procurements manager realizes the importance of correct demand forecasting and its strategic goal of efficiency and profitability

3. A marketing manager relies on the on-time delivery of design prototypes from the R&D team for forwarding to the production team

4. A sales manager understands that customer requests are a key input in product design

5. An operations manager recognizes the importance of political and economic changes on the industry

6. The operations manager notes that she must increase recruitment to meet output targets

Answer:

Option 1: This is a correct option. Understanding primary activities, such as inbound logistics and operations, in the value chain can direct your thinking in terms of how to increase value for the customer.

Option 2: This option is correct. Creating a visual representation of a value chain can help you understand the chain. It can give you a high-level view of what an organization and its various departments do in the process of creating products or services, and delivering these to customers.

Option 3: This option is correct. High-level diagrams show how different processes are connected to form an entire organization, and how various internal and external stakeholders are connected.

Option 4: This is a correct option. High-level diagrams display key inputs, outputs, and dependencies among stakeholders for each process.

Option 5: This option is incorrect. Although understanding the external environment helps build a big-picture view, it's not related to the internal value chain of the organization.

Option 6: This option is incorrect. A high-level diagram wouldn't contain sufficient information to support this kind of conclusion. However, it could, for example, make the design manager aware that her department relies on the Procurement Department to meet deadlines.

USING STRATEGIC THINKING SKILLS

Using Strategic Thinking Skills

Each person has a different way of processing stimuli, interpreting information, and reacting to situations. This is because each person has a unique mind-set. A mind-set is an established mental attitude based on your previous experiences. It determines how you process and respond to information and circumstances, and it plays a key role in the decisions you make.

To develop a strategic mind-set, you can take specific steps:

- clarify existing objectives,
- anticipate what may happen in the future,
- broaden your range of strategic inputs, and
- widen your perspective on the business and the industry you're in.

As a manager, it's vital to be able to gather and analyze complicated, and sometimes conflicting, information, and to develop sound conclusions. Often it's this skill that will determine whether you make good or bad business decisions.

As you may have noted, being able to analyze information well can have two main benefits:

- you can use the insights you gain to make good, strategic business decisions, and
- analysis can make it easier to develop valuable solutions for your department's business problems.

To use information effectively to support strategic thinking, you need to determine the kind of information to analyze; recognize possible relationships, patterns, and trends; and combine your analysis with intuition.

Determining which kind of information to analyze is crucial. If you don't, you could waste valuable time and energy on analyzing information that's irrelevant and unhelpful.

Another important part of using information effectively is the ability to recognize relationships, patterns, and trends in your area of business. Different relationships exist between different departments. Your decisions and actions may affect other departments, and vice versa.

Another way to use information effectively to support strategic thinking is to combine analysis with intuition. A useful tool for supporting strategic thinking is SWOT analysis. This involves assessing the strengths, weaknesses, opportunities, and threats for an organization or a department.

When purchasing a house, you don't generally just look at one and decide that's the best house for you. Instead you look at several houses and compare them before making your final decision. This process of choosing between various alternatives is relevant in business too. And in both cases, decisions tend to involve trade-offs. You have to weigh the advantages and disadvantages of each option, according to your priorities.

To decide which actions to prioritize, consider which are best aligned to your organization's and department's strategic vision and objectives. As an example, consider how two strategic objectives – to reduce costs and to improve brand awareness – influence a manager's decisions about which actions to pursue.

Another essential element for making effective trade-offs is to identify and evaluate alternatives. First decide what you will or won't do, because although various alternatives exist, there may be some you wouldn't want to accept under any circumstances. This prevents you from wasting time and money on alternatives you don't support or you feel won't work.

The final step for ensuring you make effective trade-offs is to balance unit and company needs. To make effective trade-offs, you need a big picture view of your organization, including knowing how your decisions or actions may affect other departments.

For instance, a product development manager wants to introduce a new product three months prior to the release date that was originally planned. Although this will be good for her business unit, it will put pressure on the Marketing Department, which hasn't finalized the marketing strategy for the new product.

Strategic thinking for functional managers means finding new and innovative ways to support the strategic goals of your organization, through the management of your own department. Creative thinking is a skill that can help you do this.

Creative thinking is a skill you can use to break away from the standard responses to business problems. You use it to develop new ideas, approach problems from a different angle, and get new perspectives on situations.

Assumptions are beliefs that haven't been proved correct. They're based on bias or personal judgment. For example, you may assume there's only one way to manage your staff, or you may simply assume the supplier you're currently working with is the best.

But assumptions can limit the way you think, preventing you from considering other alternatives. For instance, using a different management style might result in more motivated and productive staff. Or using another supplier may provide better value for your money.

It's tempting to assume there's a definite right and wrong answer to every question. With this approach, each strategic decision becomes an "either-or" choice. This limits the alternatives and potential solutions you consider. To open your mind to new possibilities, you need to learn how to view things differently. To do this, you can reframe situations and challenges, adopting a different perspective to gain new insights.

To start viewing things differently, you should be aware of your own attitude to strategic development. Do you prefer a series of small, controlled steps, or wide-ranging and extensive actions?

Curiosity is one of the driving elements of creative thinking. When people stop asking questions, they've generally stopped challenging assumptions. Sometimes this happens due to laziness. Or people may fear that asking too many questions will make them appear ignorant or weak.

Effective strategic and creative thinkers are aware that learning is a lifelong pursuit. Believing you know enough can lead to limited thinking and mediocre strategic planning. To challenge yourself to think creatively, you should aim to ask questions more than you give answers. You should aim to ask various people in your organization for their perspectives and use open-ended questions when possible.

WHAT IS A STRATEGIC MIND-SET?

What is a strategic mind-set?

Each person has a different way of processing stimuli, interpreting information, and reacting to situations. This is because each person has a unique mind-set. A mind-set is an established mental attitude based on your previous experiences. It determines how you process and respond to information and circumstances, and it plays a key role in the decisions you make.

To be an effective strategic thinker, you need to develop a strategic mind-set.

A strategic mind-set is one that can envision what an organization can and should become. And functional managers can follow through on this by developing their departments and employees in line with this vision.

Strategically-minded functional managers consider organizational goals and how these translate into departmental goals. They also take account of the future, and of the internal and external environment in which the business is operating.

Having a big-picture view of the organization is an important characteristic of strategic thinking. And strategic thinking is worthwhile because you can use it to analyze information and situations effectively, come up with creative solutions, and make good trade-offs when necessary.

Question

Which statement best describes a strategic mind-set?

Options:

1. A holistic view that assesses organizational objectives and determines how these translate into departmental objectives

2. A focus on how day-to-day tasks relate to a department's goals

3. A view that focuses solely on departmental goals and strategies and how these can be achieved as quickly as possible

Answer:

A strategic mind-set envisions what an organization and its separate departments can and should become. It considers organizational goals and how these translate into departmental goals, and takes both internal and external environmental factors into account.

DEVELOPING A STRATEGIC MIND-SET

Developing a strategic mind-set

To develop a strategic mind-set, you can take specific steps:

- clarify existing objectives,
- anticipate what may happen in the future,
- broaden your range of strategic inputs, and
- widen your perspective on the business and the industry you're in.

One step to develop a strategic mind-set is to clarify existing objectives. This requires you to understand the strategic vision and goals of your organization. If you're going to lead a department, team, or business unit in the right direction, you need to know what your organization's objectives are and translate these into departmental objectives. You need to be very clear about these objectives. Two helpful ways to do this are to ask questions and to expand on the objectives.

See each way of clarifying objectives to learn more about it.

Ask questions

To better understand the strategic objectives of your organization, ask your senior managers or organizational leaders for their interpretations. They may be able to help you understand the goals your department should be aligned with.

Also, if you're given an objective, don't make the mistake of assuming you understand it. Instead, be bold enough to ask for clarification. For example, senior management may tell you and other department leaders that the organization needs to cut costs. Although this is an objective, it's quite vague. To clarify the objective, you could ask if the cost-cutting needs to apply across all or only certain departments, and by how much costs should be cut.

Expand on objectives

As part of clarifying objectives, seek to expand on the objectives you've identified or been given. You could speak to your manager about objectives that have been set, and offer additional ideas or goals for improving results.

For example, if an organization's objective is to cut costs, you suggest it may also help to boost sales in certain areas.

Another step that can help you develop a strategic mind-set is learning to anticipate the future. To develop your ability to do this, you need to envision future challenges for your team, develop your ability to forecast, train yourself to be more attuned to the information that's available to you, and talk to a wide range of people about their views of the future.

See each aspect of anticipating the future for more information about how it helps to develop a strategic mind-set.

Envision future challenges

Envisioning future challenges might directly help you clarify your departmental objectives. For example, a new open trade policy in an emerging market can help you set clear expansion and growth goals for your sales team.

This awareness can also indirectly help you to better interpret and understand organizational objectives for your team. You can better rationalize and implement budgetary plans assigned to your department based on your analysis of competitive and cost pressures in your industry and how your corporate strategy responds to them.

Develop ability to forecast

Your skills at forecasting are important because having an idea what changes the future might bring and their effects can help you prepare for them. Forecasting may involve numbers and statistics, critical thinking, or emotional intelligence. You may also use memory and visual thinking to learn from past occurrences and patterns.

Be attuned to information

To help you anticipate the future, become more sensitive to all, and not just some, of the information you constantly receive. This includes information from television, radio, news articles, journal articles, colleagues, employees, and competitors.

Talk to range of people

Interacting with a wide age range of people can help you anticipate the future. Talk to people in a variety of age groups, with different levels of experience and expertise, as well as from different cultural or social perspectives to get their views on the future and on what's important.

Another way to enhance your ability to think strategically is to broaden the range of inputs you receive so you get as much insight as possible.

Talk to external and internal customers to get a better idea of what their wants and needs are.

For instance, a marketing manager may meet with external customers to determine what product features they like. The same manager might also meet with internal customers, such as product development managers, to find out their views on product features.

Ensure you have a wide network of individuals, both from inside and outside your organization, with whom you can discuss strategic matters. Speaking to different individuals is useful because everyone has unique insights and thoughts. Discussing these can lead to new, inspiring ideas and different understandings.

Finally, widening your perspective on the business and industry you're in will help develop a strategic mind-set. One way to do this is by creating and getting involved in different job assignments. This will challenge you in unfamiliar areas and may help you think differently.

It's also useful to involve yourself in different projects and teams that cut across functional departments or units.

For example, work in different capacities, such as operational, advisory, or even high-level planning roles. Doing this will expose you to issues you're not accustomed to dealing with. It will also help you network with individuals who manage other business units, and understand their methods and ways of thinking.

For instance, a finance manager may work on a cross-functional team comprising marketing, sales, and research and development managers to design a new product in response to an emerging demand.

Question

Which actions can help you develop a strategic mind-set?

Options:

1. Ensure you direct all your attention to projects that are a priority for your department

2. Speak to colleagues in other departments about their understanding of your organization's strategic

goals

3. Get involved in projects with other business unit leaders

4. Remain focused on the present and avoid thinking too far ahead, given that you can't predict the future

5. Send surveys out to teenagers who are part of your target market asking them how they think trends

will develop

6. Meet with other functional managers to determine their needs and how these relate to your department

Answer:

Option 1: This is an incorrect option. To develop a strategic mind-set, you should aim to widen your perspective of your business and the industry. One way to do this is by becoming involved in cross-functional projects and teams.

Option 2: This option is correct. To develop a strategic mind-set, you need to clarify the objectives of your organization. One way of doing this is by speaking to colleagues about their interpretations of your organization's goals and vision.

Option 3: This is a correct option. One way to develop your strategic mind-set is to widen your range of strategic inputs. To do this, it's useful to involve yourself in different projects and teams that cut across functional departments or units.

Option 4: This option is incorrect. Although it's true you can't predict the future, you should develop your ability to make accurate forecasts based on the information at your disposal. This can help you develop a strategic mind-set.

Option 5: This option is correct. Part of having a strategic mind-set is being able to anticipate the future. One way you can do this is by speaking to a wide range of people, including younger individuals, who may have particular insights into how trends, values, and interests will change.

Option 6: This is a correct option. To develop a strategic mind-set, you should obtain input from as wide a range of sources as possible. One way you can do this is by speaking to functional managers to determine what their needs and wants are, and how you and your department can influence these.

BENEFITS OF ANALYZING INFORMATION

Benefits of analyzing information

As a manager, it's vital to be able to gather and analyze complicated, and sometimes conflicting, information, and to develop sound conclusions. Often it's this skill that will determine whether you make good or bad business decisions.

As you may have noted, being able to analyze information well can have two main benefits:

- you can use the insights you gain to make good, strategic business decisions, and
- analysis can make it easier to develop valuable solutions for your department's business problems.

See each benefit of analyzing information to learn more about it.

Make good decisions

You can use the insights you gain through analyzing complex information to determine the best courses of action and make informed decisions.

For instance, a production line manager at a leading automobile manufacturer wants to increase production in his department. He reads industry journals and newspaper articles, and speaks with employees on the shop floor to gather information about new methods for improving production processes and productivity. He then uses this information to determine a course of action for his department.

Develop valuable solutions

Analyzing information effectively can help you develop solutions to specific problems.

For example, you're a human resources manager dealing with the problem of losing technically skilled employees who are in high demand within your industry. You evaluate this trend and realize your competitors are attracting these professionals with better offers, more recognition, and aggressive recruiting campaigns. By analyzing the feedback from professionals and competitor human resources managers, you're able to identify the problem and suggest ways your organization can reward employees, such as offering financial bonuses or time off work.

INFORMATION TO ANALYZE

Information to analyze

To use information effectively to support strategic thinking, you need to determine the kind of information to analyze; recognize possible relationships, patterns, and trends; and combine your analysis with intuition.

Determining which kind of information to analyze is crucial. If you don't, you could waste valuable time and energy on analyzing information that's irrelevant and unhelpful.

So when collecting information, assess the situation objectively and list the information needed to find a solution.

Once you're clear about what information you need, you need to be able to find it. It helps to develop an information-gathering plan.

Your information-gathering plan might include interviews with individuals inside and outside the organization, surveys, research using journals and the Internet, discussion groups, or direct observation of individuals or departments.

During this process, avoid wasting time collecting information that's already available. For instance, don't spend time gathering information if another manager has dealt with a similar situation to yours and already has the information you need.

For example, suppose customer complaints are increasing. You assess the situation objectively and realize the complaints relate to delayed product delivery times.

To provide a solution to the problem, you list the information you need to gather about the causes of the delays. You identify three key pieces of information you need to know more about.

Using the information you gathered, you can now plan your sources and enter your findings in the information-gathering plan. You speak with other managers and employees, and ask them what their thoughts are. You also observe how employees in various departments work and what they may be doing that's causing delays.

By gathering this information, you determine that outdated equipment is causing staff members to miss deadlines, which is causing delayed delivery times.

You use this information to put a proposal forward to your managers. This proposal recommends solving the problem of delayed delivery times by purchasing new equipment.

Question

An accounts manager notices missing figures and data in some of the financial reports she has to approve. The manager isn't sure if this is due to a technical fault with the software used or because of user error, and wants to determine what information to analyze.

What can the manager do to determine the type of information she needs to analyze?

Options:

1. Collect as much information as possible

2. Ask herself questions about her current situation as if she's an outsider

3. Gather information from individuals in her team, and not other managers

4. Set aside time to formulate an information-gathering plan

5. Make a list of information critical to the situation

Answer:

Option 1: This option is incorrect. When determining what information to analyze, the manager should focus on relevant data so that no resources are wasted by gathering useless information.

Option 2: This option is correct. When listing required information, the manager should view her situation objectively. This will give her a better perspective because she won't allow unnecessary details to confuse her investigations.

Option 3: This is an incorrect option. To determine what information is required, the manager should talk to different individuals from within and outside her organization. This will provide valuable information and insights from different perspectives.

Option 4: This is a correct option. As part of determining what information is needed, the manager should develop an information-gathering plan detailing the sources she'll use to gather data, such as discussion groups.

Option 5: This option is correct. It's important that the manager focus her time and effort on gathering information that's critical and relevant to solving the problem.

RELATIONSHIPS, PATTERNS, TRENDS

Relationships, patterns, trends

Another important part of using information effectively is the ability to recognize relationships, patterns, and trends in your area of business.

Different relationships exist between different departments. Your decisions and actions may affect other departments, and vice versa.

So it's important to determine how other groups function, how their work affects your department or business unit, and how your work affects them.

Try to identify patterns and trends by looking for recurring themes or events. For instance, consider the trends that two managers from different departments at a call center notice in the information they're gathering. One individual is a human resources manager and the other is a call center manager.

See each manager to learn more about how he's identified specific trends and patterns.

HR manager

The HR manager notices many call center agents are leaving the company to work for a competitor. He reviews the individuals' exit interview questionnaires to gather information about this problem. Almost all employees report the competitor offers a better pension plan and more regular employee training opportunities.

The HR manager can use the pattern he's identified to find an effective solution for restructuring benefits and retaining employees.

Call center manager

The call center manager reviews customer complaints and realizes the vast majority of complaints deal with the same issue – employees aren't able to provide the required technical assistance to their customers. The manager investigates the matter further and realizes all complaints relate to new employees.

The manager can solve the problem by providing these individuals with the necessary, adequate training.

When identifying patterns and trends, sharing information with other departments can be very useful.

For instance, in the example provided, the HR and call center managers assist one another by exchanging information about the common trends they've identified, such as lack of training among some call center agents.

Question

What actions can help you identify patterns, trends, and relationships in your organization?

Options:

1. Observe the processes other departments use

2. Review trends in your department and don't focus on those in other departments

3. Pay attention to recurring themes in the purchase behavior of key institutional customers you're assessing

4. Don't be too concerned with the functions of other departments, especially if they have different functions to yours

5. Determine how you may apply another department's best practices to your own situation

Answer:

Option 1: This option is correct. Observing the processes of other departments enables you to determine what processes they use successfully and how these can be implemented in your department.

Option 2: This option is incorrect. When identifying patterns, trends, and relationships, it helps to share your information with other managers. This cross-functional use of information can help you identify trends you weren't aware of before.

Option 3: This is a correct option. To identify trends and patterns in data, you need to pay attention to themes or circumstances that are recurring.

Option 4: This is an incorrect option. To fully understand relationships between different business units, you must determine how the functions of other units affect yours.

Option 5: This option is correct. It's important to determine how a specific approach or practice that you regard as good can be used in your situation.

ANALYSIS AND INTUITION

Analysis and intuition

Another way to use information effectively to support strategic thinking is to combine analysis with intuition.

See each concept to learn more about it.

Analysis

Analysis involves using a logical approach and breaking down complex situations or data into basic elements to better understand them. It often involves using statistics.

Intuition

Intuition refers to personal insight that isn't totally based on analytical reasoning. Often managers are faced with situations where analytical data points them in one direction, but their feelings and experience, or "hunches," point them in another. If they go with their feelings and experience, they're following their intuition.

When applying strategic thinking to situations, intuition and analysis should complement one another.

In some cases, you'll be forced to rely more heavily on intuition. For example, this happens if the factors affecting a situation are constantly changing, or when objectives or facts are unclear.

In other cases, it may be necessary to depend more on analysis of numbers, data, and facts – for instance, if you're assessing and determining a possible cost advantage.

You should allow your intuition to guide your analysis in instances where intuition is required. This involves listening to your intuition about how to react to a situation, but then verifying this through analysis to ensure you're not making the wrong decision.

For instance, a manager is meeting with a potential supplier and feels a negative energy of desperation from him.

The supplier is making many promises, but the manager feels there's something wrong and that she should consider other suppliers.

After the meeting, the manager assesses information gathered about the supplier and his company through various sources including his past customers. She realizes his company isn't doing well financially because of bad business decisions. It occurs to her the negative energy of desperation she felt was due to the supplier's effort to ensure financial survival. In this instance, she backs up her intuition with analysis and decides not to choose this supplier.

To use analysis and intuition effectively when you're faced with a decision, you should apply two additional guidelines:

evaluate the strengths and weaknesses of your options without neglecting your intuition, and avoid replacing intuition with procedures in an attempt to control uncertain situations

See each aspect of using intuition and analysis effectively to learn more about it.

Evaluate strengths and weaknesses

Sometimes it's difficult or impossible to attach numeric values to decision alternatives. For example, it may not be possible to assign values to alternatives when you're considering launching a new product into an unknown market. This is because the outcomes depend too much on unknown factors.

In cases like these, you need to evaluate the strengths and weaknesses of each alternative using your intuitive knowledge together with the information that's available.

Avoid replacing intuition with procedures

Various decisions functional managers and organization leaders make involve "gray areas" where not much reliable data is available. Many decision makers will try to control these decisions, or make them more objective, by developing and following procedures. However, it's important to note these procedures can't make up for a lack of reliable information. Instead, managers should develop and use their intuitive decision-making skills.

To use intuition and analysis to deal with situations you're facing, you also need to draw on information, insights, and experiences from past situations.

For instance, when developing new product features, a product development manager uses knowledge and experience gained during previous product development projects. The manager intuitively favors certain designs, based on what customers have reacted to well in the past and on what the latest trends appear to be.

Question

What can you do to use information in a way that supports strategic thinking?

Options:

1. Identify commonalities between different types of information

2. Use only proven procedures to make decisions, ensuring you don't let your feelings influence your judgment

3. Consider your situation from an outside perspective to determine what information you need to resolve a problem

4. Assess past experiences and use what you've learned from them to make future decisions 5. Gather information from a limited range of sources to avoid confusion

Answer:

Option 1: This is a correct option. To use information effectively, you need to be able to identify patterns, trends, and relationships. This involves recognizing commonalities, as well as differences, in different types of data.

Option 2: This option is incorrect. It may be appropriate to combine strict analysis with intuition. Relying too much on procedures can result in poor decisions, especially if the procedures aren't completely relevant given a new situation, or if the information at your disposal is incomplete.

Option 3: This option is correct. To determine the kind of information you need to analyze, you need to view an issue from an outside perspective and then identify the information required to resolve it. This objective view enables you to assess problems by viewing a larger range of information, which can help you identify things you'd miss if you maintained a subjective view.

Option 4: This is a correct option. By assessing past experiences, you're drawing on information and perceptions you can use to guide future actions. This is one way to balance intuition with analysis.

Option 5: This is an incorrect option. It's important to gather information from a wide range of sources. This prevents a limited view of the situation you're in and its possible solutions.

THE VALUE OF SWOT ANALYSIS

The value of SWOT analysis

A useful tool for supporting strategic thinking is SWOT analysis. This involves assessing the strengths, weaknesses, opportunities, and threats for an organization or a department.

See each element of a SWOT analysis for more information about it.

Strengths

Strengths in your department or organization are internal factors such as resources, abilities, and assets that improve the chances of success. To identify strengths, you can ask yourself a question like, "How does my department or organization meet and exceed the needs of different stakeholders?" The answer will give you insight about what the existing strengths are.

Weaknesses

Weaknesses are internal factors such as resources, abilities, or assets that a department or organization is missing, or that aren't being used effectively. They make it harder to achieve objectives and meet the needs of important stakeholders.

Opportunities

Opportunities are conditions or circumstances that contribute to the success of your department and organization. They can help you meet strategic objectives and are external factors.

Threats

Threats, which are external factors, are conditions or circumstances that may put your department or organization at a disadvantage and make it more difficult to achieve strategic objectives.

A SWOT analysis is valuable for strategic thinking because it prompts you to evaluate internal and external competitive environments. It should prompt you to ask various questions about these environments such as, "What value do our competitors offer that we don't?" or "How are we meeting changes in trends?"

A SWOT analysis guides strategic thinking by prompting you to adopt a big picture view of your organization and industry, as well as a clear view of where you are in relation to these.

It's valuable for strategic thinking because it also encourages active discussion between individuals to gather information.

By encouraging open conversation about strategically significant decisions, key individuals in an organization are prompted to develop new, creative ways of thinking and developing solutions. This helps individuals, departments, and organizations move away from overly restrictive thinking.

Consider how a manager uses SWOT analysis. He works for a company that provides telephonic IT support to customers and has the objective of providing customers with friendly, efficient IT support. The company is assessing different ways to meet this objective. Consider the strengths, weaknesses, opportunities, and threats that this manager identifies.

See each element of the manager's SWOT analysis for more information about it.

Strengths

The manager determines the strengths of his department and organization are quick problem response and resolution times, and highly skilled employees.

Weaknesses

The manager identifies employees' lack of proper customer and telephone etiquette as a weakness. He discusses the weakness with other managers and discovers that recent training focused on improving technical skill, not customer or telephone etiquette.

Opportunities

The manager assesses opportunities and realizes that more customers are making use of online IT assistance, as opposed to telephonic assistance. This presents an opportunity that the company could capitalize on.

Threats

The manager discovers the company's greatest competitor has launched an online support system that's accessible and easy to use. Another competitor has been rated as having the best customer service in the industry. The manager attributes this to the fact that the competitor sends staff on regular customer and telephone etiquette training courses.

By conducting a SWOT analysis, the manager is able to suggest different ways to meet the objective of providing customers with friendly, efficient IT support.

He proposes that call center agents are sent on regular customer and telephone etiquette training courses to boost customer satisfaction.

He also suggests that the company consider launching a platform through which customers can submit online support queries. This gives customers freedom of choice, and means the company is responding to the services its competitors offer.

Note, however, that the results of a SWOT analysis depend on the reliability of the information you analyze. You'll also need to practice taking the insights you've gained and putting them together to form a bigger picture.

Also remember that the real value of a SWOT analysis isn't in providing absolutely accurate data. Instead, it directs you to focus and guide your strategic thinking.

Question

What statements describe how a SWOT analysis can support strategic thinking?

Options:

1. It can be used to identify actions that can help a department meet an organization's strategic objectives

2. It enables you to assess external factors independently from internal factors

3. It helps you maintain sole focus on your department and its goals

4. It helps you determine how your business unit fits into your organization and its external environment

5. It encourages a focused way of thinking about departmental and organizational issues

Answer:

Option 1: This option is correct. A SWOT analysis gets you to examine possible opportunities and how you can use strengths identified to make the most of these opportunities, bearing in mind certain organizational weaknesses and environmental threats.

Option 2: This option is incorrect. A SWOT analysis looks at strengths and weaknesses – which are internal factors – in addition to opportunities and threats – which are external factors. This helps you maintain a big picture view of your organization.

Option 3: This option is incorrect. Besides enabling you to gain a snapshot view, a SWOT analysis also gives you a big picture view of where your department is in relation to the organization and industry you're part of.

Option 4: This is a correct option. Conducting a SWOT analysis helps you gain a clear view of your business unit, as well as a broader view of the organization and industry you're in.

Option 5: This option is correct. A SWOT analysis encourages more focused, strategic thinking by encouraging you to engage in conversations, assess circumstances, and find creative solutions to departmental and organizational problems.

TRADE-OFFS AND STRATEGIC THINKING

Trade-offs and strategic thinking

When purchasing a house, you don't generally just look at one and decide that's the best house for you. Instead you look at several houses and compare them before making your final decision. This process of choosing between various alternatives is relevant in business too. And in both cases, decisions tend to involve trade-offs. You have to weigh the advantages and disadvantages of each option, according to your priorities.

In business, making effective trade-offs is an essential strategic thinking skill. It involves looking at numerous options and determining how they relate to the big picture view of your organization. It also requires approaching all alternatives with an open mind or creative way of thinking so as to make the best decision.

For instance, a sales manager makes a trade-off between putting resources into selling an existing, popular product to an existing market and introducing a new product to a new market.

Both options are good. Selling the existing product ensures guaranteed revenue, because it's already popular. Introducing a new product may pique customer interest, and so has the potential to create revenue.

Considering the uncertain economic climate the company is functioning in, the manager decides to continue selling the existing, popular product to the existing market, as this meets the organizational priority of risk minimization.

Question

What is involved in making effective trade-offs?

Options:

1. Assessing the advantages and disadvantages of all options

2. Reviewing a couple of options to help simplify the decision

3. Considering different options and how they relate to your organization's bigger picture

4. Relying on a linear way of thinking when considering how effective alternatives are

Answer:

Option 1: This option is correct. Making effective trade-offs requires approaching all alternatives with an open mind and reviewing the related advantages and disadvantages associated with each.

Option 2: This is an incorrect option. To make an effective trade-off, you need to thoroughly assess an adequate range of alternatives.

Option 3: This option is correct. To make effective trade-offs, you need to look at numerous options so you can choose a trade-off that's aligned with the organization's goals and vision.

Option 4: This option is incorrect. Making effective trade-offs requires approaching all alternatives with a strategic way of thinking. This involves having an open mind and creative way of thinking, as opposed to a linear approach that just considers facts.

To make effective trade-offs, you can take three steps:

- prioritize the actions you take based on organizational strategy
- identify and evaluate all possible alternatives, and
- balance business unit and company needs.

PRIORITIZE ACTIONS

Prioritize actions

To decide which actions to prioritize, consider which are best aligned to your organization's and department's strategic vision and objectives. As an example, consider how two strategic objectives – to reduce costs and to improve brand awareness – influence a manager's decisions about which actions to pursue.

See each strategic objective for an example of how it might determine a manager's decision.

Reduce costs

A marketing manager has three options to meet the additional resource requirement for an upcoming launch – hiring new staff, outsourcing certain marketing activities to a subcontractor, and streamlining and reallocating resources from other campaigns.

After careful consideration, the manager decides to focus on the outsourcing and streamlining options, as these best align with the strategic objective of reducing costs.

Improve brand awareness

A marketing manager wants to promote her organization's flagship product in a new market. She needs to consider whether to put time and resources into distribution channel-based promotion, offer aggressive pricing, advertise on free social media platforms, and employ a brand ambassador to promote the organization's brand.

After some thought, she makes the decision to focus on advertising on free social media platforms and employing a brand ambassador because these are best aligned with the objective of improving brand awareness.

IDENTIFY AND EVALUATE ALTERNATIVES

Identify and evaluate alternatives

Another essential element for making effective trade-offs is to identify and evaluate alternatives.

First decide what you will or won't do, because although various alternatives exist, there may be some you wouldn't want to accept under any circumstances.

This prevents you from wasting time and money on alternatives you don't support or you feel won't work.

For instance, a product development manager is considering creating high-end, middle-market, and low-end versions of a product. He's not happy with the low-end alternative, however, because he feels it will generate lower profits.

After eliminating options that aren't worth considering, assess the pros and cons of those that remain. For instance, your company produces printers for home office users and wants to increase sales of its printers. A possible alternative for increasing the appeal of the product to consumers is to add a document scanning functionality to the printers, as a new product feature. You assess the pros and cons of this alternative.

See the pros and cons of the alternative for more information about them.

Pros

By adding a document scanning functionality as a new feature to the printers, your company can charge a higher price for the product, which is a pro. Also, the new feature may appeal to a new customer market and could improve brand awareness.

Cons

The cons of adding the new document scanning feature are that it may reduce sales for the older printers and customers may consider the new feature unnecessary. Developing a new feature would also require costly redesign.

To assess alternatives effectively, also consider the short- and long-term effects of each. For instance, a sales manager realizes sales of a product are declining and a possible solution is to reduce the price of the product. The manager assesses this option and considers its likely short-term and long-term effects.

See each effect for more information about the alternative being considered.

Short-term

The short-term effect of reducing the product price is a likely increase in sales, as customers react positively to the price cut. If the company's objective is to increase sales immediately, this short-term effect will be ideal and it's best to proceed with reducing the product price.

Long-term

The long-term effect of reducing the product price is that customers may expect similar price cuts on other company products. If these price cuts aren't forthcoming, customers may refuse to buy products until discounts are offered.

If the company's objective is to ensure continued sales over the long run without having to reduce the price of its other products, this long-term effect isn't ideal and reducing the product price isn't a good alternative to the problem.

It's also important when evaluating your alternatives to determine who'll support or oppose your ideas.

It's likely you'll receive certain support and input you absolutely require, as well as support and input you can do without.

It's therefore essential to determine who'll provide the support and input that's critical.

Question

What principles should you follow when assessing alternatives?

Options:

1. Consider both the short-term and long-term outcomes of each alternative

2. Pay more attention to the opinions of individuals who are against each alternative

3. Identify the advantages and disadvantages of each alternative

4. Be clear about which alternatives aren't worth considering

5. Trust your initial feelings when deciding which alternatives to rule in or out

Answer:

Option 1: This is a correct option. Considering the short- and long-term effects of alternatives means you're better able to anticipate outcomes and prepare adequately. For instance, anticipate and prepare for the effect that a chosen alternative has on other departments.

Option 2: This is an incorrect option. It's important, when assessing alternatives, to determine both who will support and who will oppose your particular ideas. This will help you determine which opinions to consider and which to do without.

Option 3: This option is correct. To adequately assess alternatives, you need to know the pros and cons associated with each. This makes it possible to make an informed decision that will have the most positive effect on your department and your company.

Option 4: This is a correct option. You need to determine what you will or won't do. There may be alternatives you know won't work, or that you wouldn't support. You should avoid spending resources such as time and money on these.

Option 5: This option is incorrect. It's important to consider all alternatives and their related pros and cons systematically. Alternatives that don't seem promising at first may still turn out to be worthwhile.

BALANCE NEEDS

Balance needs

The final step for ensuring you make effective trade-offs is to balance unit and company needs. To make effective trade-offs, you need a big picture view of your organization, including knowing how your decisions or actions may affect other departments.

For instance, a product development manager wants to introduce a new product three months prior to the release date that was originally planned. Although this will be good for her business unit, it will put pressure on the Marketing Department, which hasn't finalized the marketing strategy for the new product.

Releasing the product early will negatively impact the Marketing Department, which will have to put other projects on hold and speed up work on the marketing campaign for the new product. This may also negatively affect the quality of the campaign.

The product development manager's decision may also negatively affect her department's relationship with the Marketing Department.

In this instance, she'll have to consider a trade-off between generating sales by introducing the new product earlier and ensuring other departments can operate optimally.

Consider Donald, a human resources manager at a security company, who has to make a trade-off. The company's core objective is to provide highly-trained security personnel. Donald wants to hire more staff and decide on a course of action for training all security personnel.

Donald identifies what actions he'll have to take to hire new staff, in addition to the alternatives for providing training. He does this so he can determine which actions to prioritize. He realizes he must prioritize training, as opposed to hiring, and make a trade-off between two alternatives – providing in-house training or using the services of an external training agency. He decides to assess the pros and cons of each alternative.

See each alternative for information about its pros and cons.

In-house training

An advantage of in-house training is that it's relatively inexpensive because qualified individuals in the company are available to provide training.

The disadvantage, however, is that the company doesn't have adequate training materials and would have to spend money on developing these.

External training agency

An advantage of using an external training agency is that the agency provides independent certification at the end of its training program. This certification offers more market credibility than the in-house training alternative.

A disadvantage of using an external training agency, however, is that it's very costly due to the certification provided upon training completion.

Donald is willing to consider using an external training agency, but isn't willing to pay more than the industry contractor rate.

He also assesses the short- and long-term effects of each alternative. In the short term, in-house training means saving on the cost of an external training agency. However, in the long term, because of inadequate training materials, staff members won't receive the same level of training and certification obtained through an external agency, and so may need further training in the future.

The short-term effect of using an external training agency would be increased spending, but the long- term effect would be adequately trained staff who receive an independent certification and are therefore more marketable.

Other departments within the organization support either alternative.

However, it would be easier and cheaper for the Marketing Department to promote and create demand for security personnel who are trained and certified by an external, and more reputable, agency, compared to internally-trained personnel.

After evaluating his alternatives, Donald decides to trade the costs he'd save through in-house training for the long-term advantage of ensuring employees have the best possible training and certification.

Case Study: Question 1 of 2
Scenario

Eugene is a finance director. He finds himself in a situation where he has to make a trade-off.

Answer the questions in the given order.

Question

Which alternative is not aligned with the company's objective?

Options:

1. Training staff members in the Finance and Accounting Department

2. Outsourcing some processes to a third-party vendor

3. Deploying new accounting software

Answer:

Option 1: This is an incorrect option. The skills and capabilities staff members will gain through training will enable them to remain efficient in the long run. This aligns with the company's objective of improving efficiency.

Option 2: This is the correct option. Although outsourcing seems like a good alternative, it's not aligned with the company's objective of improving internal processes. This option creates a risk that the company will lose control over quality and flexibility, and it doesn't guarantee processes will be made more efficient.

Option 3: This option is incorrect. The new accounting system is more streamlined and will reduce delays in processing bills. Introducing the new system therefore aligns closely with the company's objective of improving efficiency.

Case Study: Question 2 of 2

Eugene decides the alternative of outsourcing some processes to a third-party vendor isn't aligned with the company's objective. He now has to decide between the two remaining alternatives.

Which alternative is a better trade-off in Eugene's situation?

Options:

1. Training staff members within the department
2. Deploying new accounting software

Answer:

Option 1: This option is incorrect. Training staff members will make them more efficient in the long run. However, deploying the new software is likely to make a more significant difference to the company's efficiency because the current software is causing considerable delays.

Option 2: This is the correct option. Both alternatives are good. However, deploying new software will result in greater efficiency and a reduction in errors and delays. Deploying new accounting software is quick and directly helps deliver the goals of efficiency and cost effectiveness. Although training is a good option, it takes time to deliver results and isn't as direct a method as automating processes.

INTRODUCING CREATIVE THINKING

Introducing creative thinking

Strategic thinking for functional managers means finding new and innovative ways to support the strategic goals of your organization, through the management of your own department. Creative thinking is a skill that can help you do this.

Creative thinking is a skill you can use to break away from the standard responses to business problems. You use it to develop new ideas, approach problems from a different angle, and get new perspectives on situations.

Ideally, creative thinking is a collaborative process that occurs in an environment where everyone participating feels safe to contribute and to challenge norms.

In a global market, creative thinking is especially important. Organizations compete closely with one another for a finite number of customers. Those that come up with innovative ways of meeting customers' needs are more likely to succeed.

As you may have noted, people often believe that creative thinking isn't logical enough for business purposes, or that it isn't useful in finding objective solutions to business problems. It's also common to believe that more creative approaches are impractical and will lead to uncertain outcomes.

Other misconceptions are that creative activities aren't "real work," that creative people won't be taken seriously, and that creativity is an innate skill that can't be learned.

Due to misconceptions, creative thinkers may not always be taken seriously. However, it's vital to overcome misconceptions, as creative thinking enables business thinkers adopt a fresh and dynamic approach.

Stepping outside formal and predictable business constraints can allow strategic thinkers to gain an important competitive edge.

To develop your creative thinking skills, you can challenge your assumptions, view things differently, and ask more questions.

CHALLENGING YOUR ASSUMPTIONS

Challenging your assumptions

Assumptions are beliefs that haven't been proved correct. They're based on bias or personal judgment. For example, you may assume there's only one way to manage your staff, or you may simply assume the supplier you're currently working with is the best.

But assumptions can limit the way you think, preventing you from considering other alternatives. For instance, using a different management style might result in more motivated and productive staff. Or using another supplier may provide better value for your money.

To challenge your assumptions, you need to examine your assumptions, challenge current approaches to work, welcome new ideas, and change your routines.

See each method you can use to challenge your assumptions for more information about it.

Examine assumptions

To examine your beliefs and assumptions, you need to be aware of them. You can distinguish those based on fact from those you've accepted without question. For example, why do you assume a team member is better suited for research than for meeting clients? Did you observe something in this person's behavior that made you think that way?

Once you know the origin of your assumptions, you can study them to find out if they're correct.

Challenge current approaches to work

Once you've identified your assumptions and their origins, you're ready to challenge the way you've thought about things in the past. A simple way of doing this is to list commonly-held assumptions. Then ask yourself whether you and your employees can work differently and tackle tasks in new ways.

Welcome new ideas

When you're ready to challenge your assumptions, you'll welcome new ideas. Remember, the premise of creative thinking is there isn't just one correct way of doing something. You'll have to listen attentively and avoid dismissing ideas that initially seem impractical or even irrational. You can also consult creative thinkers in your organization and use brainstorming sessions to generate new ideas for consideration.

Change routines

Challenging assumptions isn't something you do only in theory. You also need to be prepared to implement your ideas by changing your routines. You can do this by reordering daily tasks or changing your office environment to remind you that work and business processes aren't set in stone and can be easily changed.

Question

As a manager, you're setting up a new marketing division that will be responsible for promoting a new product. A creative campaign is needed.

How can you enhance your thinking by challenging your assumptions?

Options:

1. Examine the basis of your team selection
2. Look to past campaigns for inspiration
3. Adopt new approaches for routine challenges
4. Invite fresh input and contributions
5. Follow your instincts and avoid overthinking
6. Tackle your usual tasks in a new way

Answer:

Option 1: This is a correct option. The more you examine your thoughts and conclusions, the more easily you'll be able to recognize whether they're based on assumptions.

Option 2: This is an incorrect option. If you focus on past successes, you're more likely to continue making assumptions than to challenge them.

Option 3: This option is correct. One way of challenging your assumptions is by altering routines. To do this, you have to ask yourself how you could do things differently. For example, when faced with a routine task, you could ask yourself how others may tackle the task, and why. This thinking can then lead to new perspectives and a possible new approach to work.

Option 4: This is a correct option. Exposing yourself to others' ideas and perspectives is bound to challenge some of your assumptions.

Option 5: This is an incorrect option. Just following instinct at the expense of thought leaves you at the mercy of your assumptions rather than helping you to challenge them.

Option 6: This option is correct. You can challenge your assumptions and gain a new perspective by approaching mundane tasks and activities in a new way. For example, if you need to select team members for a project, you may forgo examining resumes in favor of setting up questionnaires asking potential candidates how they'd envision the completed project if they were in charge. You can then select candidates on the merit of their responses.

VIEWING THINGS DIFFERENTLY

Viewing things differently

It's tempting to assume there's a definite right and wrong answer to every question. With this approach, each strategic decision becomes an "either-or" choice. This limits the alternatives and potential solutions you consider. To open your mind to new possibilities, you need to learn how to view things differently. To do this, you can reframe situations and challenges, adopting a different perspective to gain new insights.

To start viewing things differently, you should be aware of your own attitude to strategic development. Do you prefer a series of small, controlled steps, or wide-ranging and extensive actions?

The more comfortable you are dealing with wide-ranging, extensive changes, the easier you'll find it to reframe situations.

For example, as a manager, you're presenting a project to a review board. It's possible to frame the project in two slightly different ways – both prioritizing damage control, but emphasizing different tasks. If you're comfortable with wide ranging change, you can also reframe the project in a radically different third way, presenting the damage control as an initiative allowing the company to excel.

To help you view things differently, you can ask questions to reframe the situation, work counterculturally, view challenges as opportunities, and use lateral thinking tools.

See each technique to learn more about it.

Ask questions to reframe

There are several questions you can ask to reframe situations. For example, ask how your organization would change if it did everything the customer wanted, what quality means to the organization, and how well the current organizational structure relates to the mission statement.

You can ask questions that get people to examine core beliefs and assumptions, and get them to change their perceptions.

Work counterculturally

To work counterculturally, you can change roles or suggest that others change roles. This can often lead to a fresh perspective. For example, a manager could spend a day working on a production line or at a reception desk. This change could reveal issues that aren't apparent from a managerial viewpoint, but that affect the way business is done.

View challenges as opportunities

If you treat challenges like opportunities, you'll change the way in which people approach situations. If a potential outcome is presented as potential gain rather than a loss, people will be more enthusiastic.

Use lateral thinking tools

Lateral thinking tools can open your mind to new possibilities. Lateral thinking involves shuffling your usual, linear patterns of thought. For example, it might involve using multiple, and sometimes seemingly illogical, approaches instead of following a logical sequence of one step at a time to solve a problem.

Examples of lateral thinking tools are exercises like brainstorming, storytelling, and creative visualization. These can all help a team find fresh new solutions to problems.

Question

Imagine you're a project leader who wants to renew your team's approach to work.

How can you help your team view the next project differently?

Options:

1. Ask team members to swap roles for a while

2. Revisit your best-received projects to get people to recall when they excelled

3. Hold regular brainstorming sessions and welcome all ideas, no matter how obscure

4. Reiterate the project's importance and warn of the usual potential pitfalls

5. Ask your team members questions to challenge their preconceptions about the business

6. Present possible obstacles to a new way of working as opportunities for your team to excel

Answer:

Option 1: This is a correct option. Switching roles facilitates different operational perspectives and may yield fresh insights.

Option 2: This is an incorrect option. Revisiting past glories may reinforce existing perspectives. Instead, get team members to examine how other departments or teams in other organizations work.

Option 3: This is a correct option. By using lateral thinking tools like brainstorming, you'll encourage new ideas and get people to adopt different perspectives.

Option 4: This is an incorrect option. Reinforcing old work patterns may encourage reliance on assumptions. You can reframe the situation by focusing on the positive outcomes of success rather than the consequences of failure.

Option 5: This is a correct option. By asking the right questions, you can get people to reconsider their core beliefs about their organization and their approach to work.

Option 6: This option is correct. You can get people to adopt new approaches to work by reframing challenges as opportunities. You're more likely to inspire fresh perspectives by creating a sense of positive challenge than a fear of failure.

LEARNING BY ASKING QUESTIONS

Learning by asking questions

Curiosity is one of the driving elements of creative thinking. When people stop asking questions, they've generally stopped challenging assumptions.

Sometimes this happens due to laziness. Or people may fear that asking too many questions will make them appear ignorant or weak.

Effective strategic and creative thinkers are aware that learning is a lifelong pursuit. Believing you know enough can lead to limited thinking and mediocre strategic planning.

To challenge yourself to think creatively, you should aim to ask questions more than you give answers. You should aim to ask various people in your organization for their perspectives and use open-ended questions when possible.

See each approach to learn more about it.

Ask people for perspectives

Ask various people in your organization the same questions to uncover new perspectives and ideas.

For example, a new departmental head might ask the managers of other departments for ideas on how to improve her department. She can use the answers as a starting point for new avenues of strategic thinking.

Use open-ended questions

To stimulate creative thought, you should ask open-ended questions, which prompt others to elaborate rather than providing just short or fixed answers.

An example of an open-ended question is, "What do you think is the main aim of our business?" This will yield more informative responses than a closed-ended question like, "Do you think we're in the customer service business?"

Once you've asked a number of open-ended questions, you can focus on specific concepts and start developing ideas.

When you question people, do it unobtrusively. People may become reticent or even annoyed if they feel you're becoming intrusive or wasting their time. You should also avoid wording your questions in an accusatory way. A question like, "Who knows what's causing these late deliveries?" may cause a person to become defensive. Instead it would be better to rephrase as, "Why do you think we have frequent late deliveries?" This avoids the element of blame.

Question

You're a marketing manager who's creating a campaign for a new cell phone. The current market is very competitive and you need a fresh, creative hook to sell the product.

How can you encourage yourself and your team to think outside the box?

Sorin Dumitrascu

Options:

1. Select a panel of employees and ask them open-ended questions about what they value in a cell phone
2. Verify your own assumption that the target market for this cell phone model consists of people in the 25-to-40 age group
3. Look back to a cell phone campaign you previously worked on to get inspiration
4. Follow your instincts, which have brought you good results in the past
5. Use brainstorming sessions with your team to come up with dynamic campaign ideas

Answer:

Option 1: This is a correct option. You can stimulate creative thinking by asking questions. It's ideal to ask open-ended questions and then follow up with more focused questions to develop ideas.

Option 2: This option is correct. You should challenge your assumptions to start thinking creatively. You can examine your thoughts and beliefs to determine whether they're false or based on sound logic.

Option 3: This is an incorrect option. Looking to the past might reinforce long-held assumptions. You should instead try to reframe the situation to gain a new perspective.

Option 4: This is an incorrect option. You should examine your thoughts and challenge your assumptions to avoid falling back on old ideas.

Option 5: This is a correct option. You can view things differently by using lateral thinking tools, such as brainstorming. These can help you formulate new ideas.

REFERENCES

References

Becoming a Strategic Leader: Your Role in Your Organization's Enduring Success - 2005, Richard L. Hughes and Katherine Colarelli Beatty, Jossey-Bass

Strategic Thinking: A Nine Step Approach to Strategy and Leadership for Managers and Marketers, 3rd edition - 2010, Simon Wootton and Terry Horne, Kogan Pag

Seeing the Forest for the Trees: A Manager's Guide to Applying Systems Thinking - 2002, Dennis Sherwood, Nicholas Brealey Publishing

GLOSSARY

Glossary

A

analysis - The process of examining an entity or situation using a logical approach in which complex data is broken down into basic elements.

assumption - A thought or belief that hasn't yet been proved true.

B

boundary - A physical or conceptual barrier between objects, people, or ideas.

business-level strategies - Strategies developed by middle-level managers that focus on individual strategic business units (SBUs).

C

confirmation bias - The tendency to search for information that confirms what you believe is true.

corporate-level strategies - Strategies developed by top managers that affect an organization as a whole.

creative thinking - A way of thinking that involves developing and being open to new ideas, responses, and ways of completing tasks.

F

functional-level strategies - Strategies developed by functional or department managers that relate to how business functions are carried out. They should be designed to support strategies at the business and corporate levels.

G

generative - An approach to understanding the world that requires you to incorporate seeming paradoxes and search for additional truths rather than trying to reduce the information to a single truth.

H

hypothesis testing - A scientific approach, which begins with an exploratory "What if?" question, which is followed up by an "if...then" hypothesis. Data is then analyzed to determine whether it supports the conclusion or not.

I

intuition - Personal insight – or "gut feeling" – as opposed to analytical reasoning.

L

lateral thinking - The process of using nonlinear and unorthodox thought processes to solve problems creatively.

M

mind-set - An established mental attitude or way of thinking. It determines how you process and respond to information and circumstances, and is typically developed over the course of many years.

Sorin Dumitrascu

O

operational thinking - Thinking focused on an organization's day-to-day operations, rather than on its long-term strategies. For example, operational priorities may include reducing costs, improving efficiency, and making continuous improvements to procedures within a particular department or strategic business unit.

organizational strategies - Strategies in an organization at the corporate, business, and functional levels. They define an organization's direction, including what it wants to achieve and how.

P

Porter's five forces model - A model that reviews the strength of five competitive forces in the business environment, which help to determine long-term profitability and competition in the industry. These five forces are customers, suppliers, new entrants, substitutes, and rivals.

R

reductionist - An approach to understanding the world through eliminating anything seen as invalid or contradictory, whittling the information down to a single, unquestionable truth.

reframe - The action of considering a situation or concept from a different perspective.

S

SBU - Abbreviation for strategic business unit, any division or department within an organization that maintains some independence from other parts of the organization and has its own strategies, while still contributing to the achievement of the organization's overall objectives.

SIPOC diagram - SIPOC stands for Suppliers, Inputs, Process, Outputs, and Customers. A visual map that provides an overall view of a process showing cross-functional activities.

strategic business unit - See SBU.

strategic mind-set - A way of thinking that involves constantly envisioning what an organization can and should become, and how organizational goals can be translated into departmental goals.

strategic planning - An approach to understanding and acting that takes into account context, future direction, and practical ways to achieve future-directed goals.

strategic thinking - A way of thinking that involves focusing on the big picture, identifying how each decision and activity can help support an organization's vision, mission, and goals.

strategy - The direction of an organization or strategic business unit, defining what it wants to achieve and how.

supply chain - A visual overview of the flow of goods from the supplier to the customer to help to improve efficiency and reduce waste.

SWOT analysis - An assessment of the strengths, weaknesses, opportunities, and threats for an organization or department.

systems thinking - An approach to understanding the world that involves viewing your situation or organization holistically, considering how each system works, and how subsystems interconnect within it. To do this, you need to be able to understand your actions and decisions contextually, while also being able to consider sufficient details to make appropriate decisions.

T

trade-off - A compromise in which you choose one alternative over another.

V

value - Anything that customers are willing to pay for in terms of what your organization provides.

value chain - A visual overview of what your organization does to provide benefits for your customers.

Printed in Great Britain
by Amazon

48887943R00099